Heart Connection

Science Reveals The
Secrets of True Intimacy

A book designed to help singles,

engaged, or married,

find a path to

full intimacy and marital joy.

Drs. Nancy and Ron Rockey

Also by Ron and Nancy Rockey

Belonging

Betrayed

Chosen

The Passenger

The Mode

The Route

The Destination

Heart Connection

Science Reveals The
Secrets of True Intimacy

Drs. Nancy and Ron Rockey

WESTBOW
PRESS
A DIVISION OF THOMAS NELSON

Unless otherwise noted, Scripture is taken from the Holy Bible, New
International Version®, NIV® Copyright © 1973, 1978, 1984 by Biblica,
Inc.™ Used by permission. All rights reserved worldwide.
Texts credited to the Amplified Bible are from Amplified Bible, Copyright © 1954,
1958, 1962, 1964, 1965, 1987 by The Lockman Foundation. Used by permission.
Texts credited to the RSV are from Revised Standard Version of the Bible,
copyright © 1946, 1952, and 1971 National Council of the Churches of Christ
in the United States of America. Used by permission. All rights reserved.

WestBow Press books may be ordered through booksellers or by contacting:
WestBow Press
A Division of Thomas Nelson
1663 Liberty Drive
Bloomington, IN 47403
www.westbowpress.com
1-(866) 928-1240

Because of the dynamic nature of the Internet, any web addresses or links contained in
this book may have changed since publication and may no longer be valid. The views
expressed in this work are solely those of the author and do not necessarily reflect the
views of the publisher, and the publisher hereby disclaims any responsibility for them.

Any people depicted in stock imagery provided by Thinkstock are models,
and such images are being used for illustrative purposes only.

Certain stock imagery © Thinkstock.

ISBN: 978-1-4497-1338-6 (sc)
ISBN: 978-1-4497-1340-9 (dj)
ISBN: 978-1-4497-1339-3 (e)

Library of Congress Control Number: 2011924438

Printed in the United States of America

WestBow Press rev. date: 3/22/2011

Dedicated

To John and Phyllis Rebstock
You nurtured me when my parents couldn't or wouldn't;
You loved me when as a child I was ignored.
Phyllis – you held me when my mother could not;
John – You taught me when my own father was too busy.
You stood beside me as my Best Man,
You both gave us a perfect example of teamwork,
of sacrificial love; of commitment against all odds.
Somehow the name Phyllis always goes with "John,"
and with LOVE—
and for us, it always will!
Thank you!

And

To our daughters, Sara Louise and Naomi Lynn,
And their dear husbands, Wade and Bob,
In the joy of knowing that your marriages are
based on True Heart Connections,
and in the hope that your children and grandchildren
will choose the same blessing in their lives.
When two hearts as one unite,
The load is easy, the burden is light.

Table of Contents

Illustrations

Preface

Almost everyone loves stories, and believe it or not, everyone has a story of their own. You may not have written down your story. You may not have told it or even recognized that you have one, but nonetheless, you do. Your story began long before you were born, even before you were conceived. Your story began in the lives of the generations who came before you. Carried within you is their history, as some scientists say, a "bible filled with their genetic code" from both sides of your family for at least four generations past. These stories, like the stories of people in the Bible, contain the health, characteristics, attitudes, and thoughts, the goals and dreams, the relationships and experiences of your ancestors on both sides of your family. These stories—both the good and bad from your predecessors—combine with every experience of your life to create your personal story.

Like people everywhere, your ancestors lived and worked and loved and made mistakes. Their lives were influenced by *their* ancestors, and how *they* lived. The good news is that you are not destined to repeat their inherited and cultivated tendencies. Today's cutting edge science is unlocking mysteries in God's Word that that have not been well understood before. As you learn these "secrets," these, combined with your willingness, can truly alter your destiny.

"I know the plans I have for you," declares the Lord, "plans to prosper you and not to harm you, plans to give you hope and a future" (Jer. 29:11).

When you met and "fell in love" both you and your significant other thought that things were pretty simple. You loved each other and that was all you needed. Isn't that what we've been taught to believe? Each of you holding this book in your hand has a story of the relationship with the person of your choice. You may be engaged to marry, or you may have been married for half a century, but regardless of the length of your relationship it has its own history, its own nuances that make it different from everyone else's. And yet a similar thread runs through all liaisons—they all have their ups and downs, their successes and their challenges. And each person involved wants their connection with the love of their life to be like a fairytale romance, the content of a great novel, the account of the greatest love in human history. But not all relationships are like that. In fact, most are almost nothing like that. For it's not true that "love is all your need." If it were, would there be so many broken promises, unhappy people, and fractured families?

We (Nancy and Ron) look back on our own personal love story and see it as a terrific testimony of divine intervention—which was its only hope! During Year 12 of our life together our ongoing battle reached a fever pitch, and out of that crisis grew, at last, *a transformation to peaceful harmony*. Does that sound easy? Well, it wasn't. It was not without bloodshed (not actual), pain, suffering, and tears. Many other couples have chosen the "road less travelled" to a peaceful destination—a harmonious relationship—and the traveling wasn't easy for them either. No marriage worth having is without personal effort, introspection, responsibility taking, cooperation, and a whole lot of guidance from Above.

Does this seem like too much work? Why not just "go with the flow" and "let the chips fall where they may"? Bad idea! a marriage built on that model quickly gets the loving couple out of their initial dream-world and into a life of misery.

This book is filled with stories—true stories. Stories of pain and persistence, struggle and near disaster, stories of miracles, and of great triumph. But why so many *stories?* Why not just get to the point? Because everyone—including you—has a story. The story of their childhood, their loves and losses, their hopes, dreams, and disappointments, their friendships, their marriages. More than just telling the stories, however, we will offer the set-up behind each one and the principle that must be learned in order for the story to have a positive conclusion. In addition, we will give you both the latest in science *and* the biblically sound psychological principles that will teach you what *you* need for a fulfilling relationship.

Of course, not all people are interested in harmony and happy endings. Some are more invested in being right than being happy! Some are too stubborn, too hardened to even glimpse inside themselves for what they might have contributed to a faltering marriage.

Most relationships that fail do so because the partners want what they want, when they want it, and refuse responsibility for their part in the demise of joy. Self is on the throne and stubbornly refuses to step down, to compromise, to admit fault, to submit to the chisel that God often must use to chip away at personal dysfunction, to give us a peek at our history and cause us to see the whole truth about ourselves. And when some of us come face-to-face with these realities, we prefer finger-pointing more than understanding and forgiveness.

Let's open the pages of the Old Testament of the Bible. Look over my shoulder and hear God speaking to one of His prophets, Hosea. God is describing what He sees in the lives and actions of His people and what He sees the condition of the nation and even of the land to be. He is very concerned, and He makes it clear that there is no faithfulness, no love in the land; the people are committing acts of adultery and violence. He says that even the land mourns because of their behaviors. And then God sums up the cause of it all in these words: "My people are destroyed for lack of knowledge" (Hosea 4:6).

Today we'd say, "It's what you don't know about yourself that will drive you crazy." Lack of personal knowledge can drive you crazy alright, but it can also be the cause of much relational suffering. How many of us know much about the four generations of relatives who lived before us? How many of us can describe the relationships between our grandparents and their parents, our great-grandparents. How many of us know the secrets that have been kept "under wraps" for years and years. In many cases, those unknown secrets, those strained or explosive relationships are contributors to the frustrations we currently endure.

When we begin to learn the principles of human development and behavior, when we are courageous enough to apply that information to ourselves, the ah-ha's, the awakenings that we experience, are the beginnings of changing our relationships from misery into harmony—and even our good relationships into great ones.

If you continue in this book, if you are courageous enough to read each chapter, answer each question as it is posed, and share honestly with your mate what you discover about yourself, and when you do the work of applying these principles to your daily experience, your relationship will be way down the "road less travelled" to personal and marital harmony.

Are you ready?

OK. Get set! GO!

Introduction

Relationships are absolutely necessary for any of us to survive, learn, work, love, be loved, and procreate. These capacities are pre-programmed by the Creator into our computer-like brains and instilled in our hearts during our in-womb months. And beyond this, new science tells us great and insightful information about the programming of our genes.

Your brain, each component of it from brain stem to the cortex, has one or more specific functions. And each human brain contains the necessary ability and design to enable us to connect with others. And here's something that science is just beginning to understand: the human *heart* has a far greater capability than simply pumping life-giving, oxygen-containing blood through our bodies. It is also a component in the connections between individuals - heart to heart.

As our life progresses beyond the womb, we begin to unconsciously (that is, without conscious thought or choice) use the heritage we've received and our experiences in the womb as foundational templates through which our future relationships are formed.

Within the inner circle of intimate family and friends, we bond to each other with a type of emotional glue. The extent to which a child's needs are met will determine the type of "emotional glue" he or she will use to attach to significant others in life. Even though every child attaches to his/her caregivers, not all of the attachments are of a kind that will insure optimal heart-to-heart connection.

In childhood and onward through the years, some people seem to be naturally capable of intimate love relationships, and from their many intimate and caring relationships experience a great deal of pleasure. Others, however, don't have this at all. Some seem to feel no "pull" to form intimate relationships, and find little or no pleasure in being close to or even in the company of others. They have few, if any, friends, and their relationships with family are more distant. The "emotional glue" that holds their relationships together is a different type than that of those who form close emotional ties.

This capacity and desire to form emotional relationships begins early, while a child is still in the womb. The mother's ability to connect emotionally with her unborn child greatly influences the formation of the child's capacity to connect. And every mother's capability is impacted by the way *her* parents bonded to her as an infant and by the relationship she has with the child's birth father. The same is, of course, true of the father. Studies abound and experts agree that the parental relationship during gestation has a profound effect upon the unborn child the mother carries.

These early experiences, even before birth, and then in our first two years of life, set the stage for our future marriage. What we absorbed during those early days becomes a kind of filter through which pass all the relationships that we form and greatly influences how we feel, think, and act in them. We are even set up for the kind of person to whom we will be attracted. Perhaps he looks like your dad, or maybe she is as loving and gentle as your mom. It could even be that the negative characteristic of a parent or sibling with whom you were raised will become the model of the kind of person you will marry.

Think about your own choices. You don't believe it? Just wait and see!

CHAPTER ONE

The Great Attraction

Nancy: Today is November 30. A cold blustery wind howls around downtown corners, just like it did on this day in 1964. The chill of today, however, is warmed by the comfortable changes in my life during the nearly past five decades. "That was then, this is now," I tell myself. A shiver at the recollection makes me wish for a cup of hot tea and a cozy corner with my best friend. I wonder if Phyllis, whose birthday is today, is thinking about how life-changing this day was to her brother Ron and to me. My memory is vivid!

I had ventured out in a blinding blizzard from the university where I was studying and working. I was in a borrowed car with bald tires and a poorly functioning heater, and hoped that the gasoline supply would get me halfway – at least to an Oasis on Chicago's Skyway. Michigan's blizzards can be frightful, and this was one of the worst I'd ever seen. Snow pelted the windshield in huge flakes, making visibility very poor. The station wagon's heater groaned as it struggled to keep up with the wind and freezing temperatures. With every muscle tensed, I maneuvered past abandoned vehicles stuck in ditches, thanking God that I wasn't in one of them. Finally I spotted the toll booth ahead, up a little hill and around a slight curve.

Suddenly a gust of wind hit the driver's side of the station wagon and in horror I felt it slide to the right, off the road, and onto the shoulder's slushy decline. The brakes were useless, and in fact, touching them made me glide

1

even further off the edge. As the car came to a stop in a gully I burst into tears and pounding the steering wheel in frustration, cried out, "Why me, Lord?" After all, I was making this awful trip to Milwaukee for some counsel about a failing relationship with my fiancé. I felt so desperate about my situation that I'd determined to go for help despite a long drive in this crazy blizzard.

"Please help me Lord!" I cried and slowly and softly the instruction came to me. Putting the car in gear, I lightly touched the accelerator then slowly steered the car sideways up the embankment and onto the pavement. At last I stopped right at the tollbooth.

"You're a lucky young lady!" the attendant exclaimed. "When I saw you float off the road I thought you'd be crawling here to the booth. Certainly not driving that car!"

In the moments I sat at the toll gate I argued with myself about the wisdom of continuing the journey. I had another 200 miles ahead of me, and that included going through or around Chicago. Regardless, driven by emotional pain, I took the toll-way ticket and ventured back into the whiteout.

Nine hours later, exhausted and relieved, I arrived at the home of my childhood pastor and his family. They were shocked that I had indeed come the distance, sensed my exhaustion level, and suggested a hot shower and a cozy bed. As I crawled beneath the sheets in Carolyn's bed, I thanked God for the protection He had given me and fell quickly into a fretful sleep.

The next morning dawned too soon, and with it the invitation to go with the pastor and his wife, Uncle Joe and Aunt Hazel, to a courtroom. I accepted the invitation and on the way heard the story of why we were heading there. They'd been corresponding with a young man who had been in prison in Tennessee. He was now in Milwaukee awaiting trial for charges occurring prior to the Tennessee imprisonment. They were going to court as—believe it or not—character witnesses. His three months in the local jail had given them the opportunity to have many visits with him, and they were impressed with what they saw. He had become a Christian inside the walls of the Tennessee State Prison.

About two hours later I found myself being introduced to and shaking hands with the gentle young man who'd just been released, and who had caused my heart to literally leap when he entered the courtroom. Half an hour after that, in the pastor's car, he asked me how many children I wanted. The attraction between us was so strong that all thoughts of my fiancé literally flew away into the wind! Unfortunately, our encounter was short-lived.

I returned to the university a day later, fully intending to be responsible enough "fix" the problems with my fiancé and move on to marriage. That was however, not to be. I couldn't fix him. He didn't want to be fixed, and I didn't know what needed to be fixed in me. We parted as friends and he left for his geographically distant family. I returned to Milwaukee to my "other parents" to "get away" for a weekend. And there began the brief courtship between Ron and I and our marriage just seven months later. We were opposites, so strongly attracted to each other that nothing or no one could keep us apart!

What attracted Nancy to Ron and Ron to Nancy? Why was the attraction instantaneously so strong, and overwhelming to them both? What had set up this magnetism?

Nancy: Ron and I came from very different backgrounds. I was born into a British home where I was very much wanted by my mother, father, and grandparents; a home where warmth and affection was present most of the time. Even though my mother's pregnancy with me came at a time when my parents were separated because of the military draft and the subsequent second Great War, it was still considered a miracle and my birth eagerly anticipated. After my birth, my mother and I went to live with my maternal grandparents where I received a great deal of positive attention.

There was a three-month period during that time that Mother and I went to be with my father before he was shipped overseas and into the war. While they were together, Mother again became pregnant. My baby brother was born and died while my father was still overseas. It was in that tragedy that a "black cloud" descended upon my family. Grieving for my brother and the absence of my father took a great physical and emotional toll on the family, especially on my mother.

My father had very little interaction with me until after the end of World War II when he came home from Europe and opted out of the military. At that point, I had already lived several years without him. While he very much wanted his little girl, he treated me the way he had been treated when he was a child—very harshly. He was verbally cruel and demeaning in stark contrast to the way I'd been treated by my mother and grandparents. So basically, my father and I rejected each other.

Ron: I, on the other hand, was an unwanted child. My parents had decided, because they could afford no more, that the three children they had were more than enough. It was on a weekend trip home from the shipyard where my father worked, that I was conceived. Because my father was an explosively angry and extremely jealous man, mother decided to abort the baby. When the abortion attempt failed she went into denial that she was pregnant and held the on to the "secret" of her pregnancy for months.

At the end of her tenth month, I was born in the attic. The delivery was very difficult and Mother was taken to the hospital where she remained for weeks. My 9-year-old sister, Phyllis, became my primary caregiver. When Phyllis was in school, a 16-year-old neighbor girl cared for me. When Mother was finally discharged from the hospital she moved a couple of hundred miles away to be with my father as she continued to recover.

Women came and went in my earliest years. No caretaker was consistent, except perhaps for Phyllis. In order to get my basic needs met (food, cleanliness, and comfort), I had to scream in my crib for long periods before I got attention.

Calling me by my nickname, Phyllis describes my early years as "nobody- wanted-Butch." I was just an inconvenience, and remained so throughout my childhood and adolescence.

Points to consider: Ron

1. Ron was unwanted; an accident, so to speak.
2. Ron's mother attempted to abort him.
3. Ron's mother did not connect emotionally with him while he was in the womb.
4. Ron's birth was difficult; he weighed 10 ½ pounds.
5. Ron's birth mother abandoned him (due to illness).

Points to consider: Nancy

1. Nancy was a wanted child.
2. Nancy's mother connected strongly to Nancy while she was in the womb.
3. Nancy's birth was considered to be normal.
4. Nancy went home from the hospital to three loving and affectionate adults.
5. Nancy's father abandoned her due to WW II.

Why does this history matter? What can we learn from it?

Principle 1: We are set-up in the womb and in the first two years of life for the way we will live life and connect to others. It is then that our developing brains, like sponges, absorb everything that is seen, heard, smelled, tasted, and felt around the infant. Tension between parents, an absent parent, rejection and/or being ignored, negatively impact the developing child.

"The news from the world class laboratories at Yale, Princeton, Rockefeller and elsewhere is breathtaking in scope. Starting from the moment of conception, a child's brain is wired by his or her environment. Interaction with the environment is not merely one aspect of brain development, as had been thought; it is an absolute requirement, built into the process from our earliest days in the womb" (Pre-Parenting, p.7, Thomas Verny, M.D. and Pamela Weintraub).

From the earliest moments after conception, chemicals and hormones in the mother's body control the embryo's, the fetus's and the infant's genes—and these results can last a lifetime. The daily input from parents of consistent love and affection, can protect the child from negativity and even the tendency to see the world through gray glasses of sadness and doom.

". . . maternal feelings and moods are linked to hormones and neurotransmitters that travel through the bloodstream and across the placenta to the developing brain of the unborn child. Prolonged exposure to stress hormones, including adrenaline and cortisol, prime the growing brain to react in fight or flight mode—even when inappropriate—throughout life. Maternal emphasis on joy and love, on the other hand, bathes the growing brain in "feel good" endorphins and neurohormones such as oxytocin, promoting a life-long sense of well-being." Pre-Parenting, p. 38.

Through their influence, the genes are turned on and off, thus affecting the way that the child develops. Wolf Reik of the Babraham Institute, and Michael Skinner of the University of Washington, state that the genes are similar to the Bible, in that everything is "written down" in a code.

Not everything in the Bible is written in code, but the above scientists were referring to portions of the Bible that seem to be in code. Scientists have made great strides in deciphering the genes' code, and hope to be able to read them as we would read the Book of Life.

Many scientists, including Marcus Pembrey of University College in London, England, Randy Jirtle of Duke University, and Jean-Pierre Issa of the world famous M.D. Anderson Cancer Center, have discovered that different sets of genes produce differing physical and emotional characteristics in the offspring, dependent on the origin of the genes, maternal or paternal. "Tags" attached to the genes have the capability of tightening or loosening the genes, which turns the gene either on or off, thus affecting how the genes impact our cells.

Moshe Giff and Michael Meaney of McGill University, and others, have determined that the cells differ because of another component known as an epigene, which switches genes on and off. A gene can be compared to a computer's hardware, while the epigene is the software, telling the hardware (the gene) what to do.

While you were just an embryo, developing in your earliest stages in the womb, certain switches needed to be thrown on or off during specific time periods. The genes' being on or off determines the activity and even the destiny of the body's cells.

Confused yet? You are probably asking why in the world all this scientific jargon is in a book on marriage. Right?

Honestly, there's a reason. It is true that we are fearfully and wonderfully made, and we thank God for that. We also thank Him for the late-breaking science that confirms how detailed and meticulous God was when He created you. And beyond that, there is, because of modern science, clear evidence that *even how our genes express themselves can be changed* or recovered, substantiating the Word of God. Here is a fascinating example.

In the article, "Genomic Counter-Stress Changes Induced by the Relaxation Response," Harvard Medical School professor, Herbert Benson, M.D. says "Now we have found how changing the activity of the mind can alter the way basic genetic instructions are implemented. The mind can actively turn on and turn off genes" ("The Public Library of Science, PLoS ONE," Feb. 12, 2008). Blood samples of 19 people who had regularly prayed or meditated for years were compared with blood samples from 19 people who did not regularly pray or meditate. The research showed that those who regularly prayed/meditated suppressed more than twice of the stress-related genes than those who did not. It was also shown that stress genes could be suppressed by the non-praying/meditating group after eight weeks of ten minutes a day of prayer/meditation, but not to the extent of those who had practiced this for years.

The Bible tells us that we must change. That we must get rid of our resentments and bitterness (see Eph. 4:31), yet many of we saints argue that we can't change, that "It's just the way I am." But the Bible gives many examples of people who were changed by the power of God *and* their willingness to be changed. David, Peter, and Saul come immediately to mind, but there are numerous others, including Jacob's ten sons, led by Judah, who sold their brother Joseph into slavery and later repented to the place where Judah offered himself up to lifelong slavery in place of his youngest brother (see Gen. 44:18-33).

The fact is, we're not stuck in cement. We're not bound to the behaviors, or in many cases, even to the physical illnesses we have developed from our mental and emotional wounds. Regardless of one's beginnings in the womb, in infancy, and in those first seven character-forming years, our genes can be transformed. What it takes is knowledge, determination to heal emotionally, and the power of God for the process.

During Ron's in-womb experience, his very existence was denied. His mother did not connect emotionally with him and the tension between his parents who were mostly absent from each other, was palpable. According to his sister, after birth he had to scream and scream in order to get his basic needs met.

Dr. Verny writes: *"The physiological events of birth are charged with emotional and symbolic power. The circumstances of our birth provide the material from which we create our primary life scripts, which from deep within our minds will exert a gravitational pull on all our thoughts and actions for the rest of our lives"* (p. 78).

The events of the birth experience, difficult or easy, added to the filters in the genetic code, create the glasses through which we will view and interpret the world and our life in it. Early on, Ron learned three counterfeit lessons which haunted him until his recovery began and which occasionally still pop up in his feeling or thinking, especially if he is tired. However, because he has the tools to use and the experience of their effectiveness, it is comparatively easy for him to dismiss them.

Lessons Ron learned in childhood:

Lesson 1: Don't ever trust a woman because they will leave me.
Lesson 2: Men are not to be trusted because they are violently angry and ignore me.
Lesson 3: Don't count on anyone for what I want or need, because for sure, no one will offer to give me my needs or desires.

Nancy's in-womb experience, like Ron's, was without the constant presence of her father because he was in the U.S. Army. His voice, his touch, his tenderness with her mother during the prenatal months was missing, therefore when he did return from war Nancy was not acquainted with his presence or his characteristics. He was a stranger and his ways were unfamiliar. Her parent's relationship, while good when they had been together, was difficult now because of their long separation. The year after Nancy's birth, her mother became pregnant again, just before her husband was sent to war—the front lines in Europe. Nancy's brother was born and died before her father returned from war.

Early in Nancy's life she also learned counterfeit lessons:

Lesson 1: Men are not trustworthy. They will abandon me.

Lesson 2: When men are around, they reject and criticize me. One minute they love me and the next they abuse me, physically or emotionally.

Lesson 3: I am to be subservient to men—take any abuse they dish out, because as a female I am inferior and I deserve to be abused.

> **Implicit:** Not stated but understood, absolute (not affected by doubt or uncertainty, and present as a necessary part of something.
>
> **Implicit Memories** – formed before we have language. They impact thoughts, feelings and behaviors throughout life.

Valuable Information:

According to Dr. Daniel Siegel in his book *The Developing Mind*, memories that are formed before we have language to describe the situation or label the feelings, are called **implicit** memories. These memories are retained in the mind and, according to many scientists, in the cells of our body. They affect our attitudes, feelings, and thoughts, thus dictating our behaviors. This happens when something in our current situation intersects with an implicit memory, and we experience them as a deluge of feelings, but they are without the recognition that we are remembering anything. The reason for this is that **implicit memory** involves parts of the brain that do not require conscious processing during encoding or retrieval. Siegel further states that by a child's first birthday, repeated patterns of implicit learning are deeply encoded in the brain. When these memories are not noticed or identified, they can create turmoil in our relationships, especially intimate or marital.

Let's site an example here from Nancy's preverbal days. You'll recall that in infancy and early childhood, her father was seldom around because he was in the military, and it was during World War II. Nancy was not quite two years old when her father was sent to Advanced Medic raining in Mississippi. She and her mom were allowed to meet him in Mississippi, and so they took the train from Connecticut. arriving there, they were met and taken to the tiny one-bedroom apartment that would be their home for the next three months.

At Nancy's bedtime that first night her mother carried on with the ritual to which they had become accustomed (deeply encoded in Nancy's brain) even though they were now in a strange environment. After Nancy's bath, Mother took her to her bed where, snuggled together, Mother began reading her a story. What had always happened before was that during this comfortable and comforting time Nancy would fall asleep. Then her mother would pick her up and take her to her crib where she would sleep all night.

But on this night everything changed.

Nancy's dad wanted to be in the bed with his wife, so he picked up his young daughter and took her into the living room to the crib. Nancy was frightened. This man was almost a stranger, and she was panicked by being taken away from Mother. Crying, Nancy sat up in the crib. Her father pushed her down. She sat up again. Dad pushed her down again. This exercise was repeated so many times that her father finally pulled up a chair and sat down. Crying continually, Nancy popped up as soon as she was pushed down. She was confused and afraid. She wanted her mother. But her mother did not come, and each time she sat her father pushed her back down.

Finally after countless sit-ups, Nancy dropped into an exhausted sleep. Triumphant, her dad returned to his wife and announced: "There, I've broken her will." That lesson was quickly learned by Nancy and so were a few others later in her life.

After three months together, Mother and Nancy returned home as Jim was being shipped off to the front lines of the war. Ena was pregnant again, and for the next few months joy and expectation filled the home. But it was to be short-lived. Ena went into labor a month early and little Jimmy was born, a 4-pound, 10-ounce preemie, but in good health. Ena, on the other hand, had endured a traumatic delivery, and it was now discovered that she had infectious hepatitis. Baby Jimmy was, as preemies often are, a slow feeder, so was tube fed in the nursery. During one of those feedings, the tube was inserted into his lungs rather than into his stomach, and he drowned in the formula he was being fed.

Ena went home to her parents without her new baby. Then he was brought to them in his little coffin for the final good-byes. Now incredible sadness filled that household! Jim was in the thick of the war and little Jimmy was dead. Simultaneously, Nancy's paternal grandfather, who lived four miles away, was dying of cancer. His wife had declared that Jim, Ena, Nancy, and her maternal grandparents were enemies, because they had become members of a church she didn't approve of because it wasn't the church in which her son had been raised. Not only did sadness and mourning fill the home's atmosphere, but also the resentment and criticism of Nancy's paternal grandparents. The air was filled with tension and criticism as her grandfather's death then occurred, adding more angst and sadness to her home environment.

Nancy reports: "In my recovery process, I began to understand the reasons why a dark cloud seemed to hover over me, and my outlook, my view of the world was of sadness. That sadness had been felt in my early years, long before I had the words to express it or the vocabulary to identify my feelings. In my childhood home, feelings were not allowed anyway. 'You can't count on feelings; they mean nothing,' I often heard. 'And anyway, she's only a child. What does she know?'

"So in those *pre-verbal months*, I learned some additional mandates that seem to have channeled my thinking and behaving in subsequent years:

- You may have feelings, but you aren't allowed to identify or express them.

- Life is basically sad. There may be moments of happiness or joy, but they last only briefly. Don't get used to them.

Did these implicit memories impact my life in any way? Most definitely!

"I recall vividly (an explicit memory) the night before our wedding when Ron was leaving my family home to stay elsewhere (so he wouldn't see the bride before the ceremony). My parents stood with him at the door asking if he was sure that he wanted me, if he was REALLY going to show up at the church, or was he going to leave us all standing expectantly with him far gone from the wedding scene. After his assurances that he would be at the church, I locked myself in the bathroom, climbed in the tub, and sobbed. I felt betrayed by my own parents and just a bit fearful of the next day's event. In this situation, my recalled feelings stemming from implicit memories added to the current experience to create my devastation.

"After our marriage, still the fear of his leaving did haunt me for some time, until he did leave when I was pregnant for our second child. His issues of rejection (both implicit and explicit memories) were fueling that behavior. Add to those his fear that my ill-health may result in my death, or his fear that after baby number two was born I would no longer need him."

Lessons Repeated:

Feelings are bad – don't express them. "I spent the first 12 years of our marriage not sharing with Ron how I was feeling. I feared he would leave or that what I shared would escalate into an excruciating fight, so I stayed silent, except to repeatedly tell Ron of my love for him. However, my unexpressed feelings turned into physical illness, as they often do, further escalating Ron's fear of loss."

Life is basically sad. "It hasn't been until recently that I have come to grips with my negative perceptions, and with the knowledge that I have seen the world through gray tinted glasses for most of my life. While I have been able to put on rosy colored glasses for others to see, as I did throughout childhood, my internal thinking and feeling were true to the gray lenses I wore. I now recognize that my early implicit memories of loss and sadness during the World War II had set the stage for future years."

Memories that are retained and are formed after we have vocabulary and the ability to express them are called **explicit** memories. In Dr. Daniel Siegel's book, *The Developing Mind*, he states that when people refer to the generic idea of memory, they are speaking of explicit memory. When explicit memories are retrieved, (one has) the internal sensation of "I am remembering." Explicit memory is often communicated to ourselves and to others in the form of descriptive words or pictures communicating a story or sequence of events. Being asked to recall a sad memory, would mean that <u>you know you are remembering</u> an event and you know why you are sad.

> **Explicit:** <u>Clear, obvious</u>—<u>leaving no doubt</u> as to meaning; <u>definite</u>—not implied or guessed at.
>
> **Explicit Memories:** are retained and formed after we have vocabulary.

Ron: Let's look at one of my memories. It involves one of my brothers, George. George was eight years my senior, and had become the scapegoat of the family. He was regularly beaten down in the basement's furnace room, usually for things for which he'd already been punished, or for some "minor infraction," as I saw it. I can picture it clearly. One night I went to bed, and George arrived in our shared bedroom shortly thereafter.

Obviously he'd just had after yet another beating. George, bleeding and blistered, lay in his bed, rolling from side to side, holding himself and groaning in pain. Then, because his groaning was disturbing our oldest sister in the next room, she came in our bedroom and hit George on the head with her high-heeled shoe, trying to shut him up."

Now that's an explicit memory, clearly and visually recalled, and packed with emotion.

What did Ron learn from that experience?

Lessons Ron Learned:

<u>Rage against women</u> accompanies the memory because usually Ron's mother sat on the basement steps egging Dad on to beat George harder and longer for things he'd already been punished for. Then there was that older sister who used her high-heeled shoe to shut him up. Women can and *do* betray you.

<u>Anger at his father and sadness for his brother</u>. There's also the question that plagued Ron for years: why did Dad beat George and didn't even touch him? What was so bad about Ron that Dad wouldn't have anything to do with him?

Do you think that this **explicit memory** had any bearing on Ron's behaviors in later years? Here's how he sees it played a part in his thinking, feeling, and behaving:

Lessons Repeated:

- *Distrust for women.* "I was not sure I should trust Nancy, even after we married and for quite a few more years. I had learned that women betray you—a hard lesson to eliminate from my thinking. That fear of women, orchestrated many of my behaviors in our early troubled marriage."

- *Anger at his father.* "My father died when I was 16. My fear and suspicion of women even caused me to think that my mother had caused my father's death. It used to be that when behaviors that I had observed in my father showed up in my own everyday thinking or behaving, my resentment for Dad would escalate. Now since my recovery began some time ago, I can look back at my father with sadness, recognizing that my father's early life must have been torturous."

- *Concern for his brother.* "George's life was one of extreme unhappiness, repeated incarcerations, and emotional isolation. George remembered that at age 12 he decided that he would never allow another human to get so close to him that he would get hurt as badly as he had been hurt on that particular day."

In their adult years, when their mother died, George disappeared and no one in the family heard from him or knew his whereabouts for 12 years. Ron's remembered sadness for his brother led him to search for and find him. George was living in a senior residence home. He had endured both six-place and four-place bypass surgeries, and had already had two surgeries for cancer. He was a shadow of his former 6-foot, 6-inch frame. George was thrilled to see Ron and was happy to receive the book *Belonging* and the recovery program *Binding the Wounds*.

George's subsequent reading and studying gave him an understanding of himself *and* the ability to change his thinking and his behaviors. George died with the knowledge that he was loved and cared for, and that's what Ron wanted to provide for George.

Principle 1: As humans, we are attracted to our emotional equal.

It is hard to comprehend, but true nonetheless, that all of us have been wounded to a greater or lesser extent. It may have been your parents who wounded you, blatantly or overtly, but you can be quite sure that their intent was not to deliberately hurt you. It would be more probable that the wounds they caused were due to their doing the only thing they knew, possibly what they'd learned from their own childhoods. Perhaps the way they disciplined, or perhaps the word should be "punished" you, was a copy of the way they were treated by their parents. It also may be that the wounds you received were from others—siblings, teachers, kids on the school ground. Regardless of their origin, wounds still hurt! The old saying that "sticks and stones may hurt my bones but names will never hurt me," is a lie. The truth is that often negative, put-down words are more detrimental to one's soul than is a severe spanking.

The wound(s) you received may differ from those that your mate received. The perpetrators may have been in different relationship to you, but the level of pain is pretty much equal to that of your mate, and the need for recovery from that wound is equally important.

We marry our emotional equals because they feel like they are on the same emotional level as we are, and thus offer a sense of normality.

Somehow, after settling into marriage, we get the idea that our mates are at total fault for the angst in our relationship, but this is far from true. Each individual must look in the proverbial mirror to discover there, after in-depth examination of their own issues, the junk that they brought into the relationship. As was stated in the preface, we have been influenced by at least four previous generations on both sides of our families. How in the world could we then escape having some form of dysfunction?

Principle 2: Our in-womb and birth experience is the filter through which we interpret what we experience for the rest of life.

Dr. Thomas Verny, a psychiatrist, has devoted his career to researching and understanding the experiences of the baby in the womb and then determining the effect of those experiences of on the life of the child turned adult. He states on page 38 of his book, Pre-Parenting: *"maternal feelings and moods are linked to hormones and neurotransmitters that travel through the bloodstream and across the placenta to the developing brain of the unborn child. Prolonged exposure to stress hormones, including adrenaline and cortisol, prime the growing brain to react in fight or flight mode— even when inappropriate— throughout life. Maternal emphasis in joy and love, on the other hand, bathes the growing brain in 'feel good' endorphins and neuro-hormones such as oxytocin, promoting a life-long sense of well-being."*

To say the least, Ron's in-womb experience was very difficult. Obviously he was unwanted, as demonstrated by the attempted abortion. The stress his mother felt as she denied Ron's existence for fear that her husband would accuse her of having an affair, flooded his body with caustic hormones. The stress hormones he received set him up to experience rejection at a very deep level, honestly believing that no one would ever want him. He spent years looking for rejection under every rock, and if he didn't find it, he would manufacture it. (That's what rejected people do.) By his attitudes and behaviors he set up others to reject him. For Ron, as well as for others who have felt and have experienced prenatal rejection, getting past the old feelings has taken years of work and determined effort. Acquiring knowledge is the first step in the process of recovery and for sure, Ron has spent years *acquiring knowledge, applying it to himself* and taking the *active resolve* steps necessary to *alleviate the cause of his pain.*

The Birth Experience:

Dr. Chairat Panthuraamphorn, an obstetrician at the Hua Chiew General Hospital in Bangkok and an expert on birth explains:

"Inside the womb, fetuses can hear their mother's body noises at 72 decibels, feel warmth and gain familiarity with her heartbeat and voice. At birth they hear screaming from the mother, phones ringing from the nurse's station, the bleep, bleep of the fetal monitor, shouting sounds like 'push, push!' or the loud conversation of the health team. These delivery room sounds are noisy and inappropriate. A baby's birth under these circumstances is like bringing an individual from a rural area to the center of New York City with all its traffic and machinery" (Ibid. p. 70)

Considerable research has been done regarding the effects of a difficult delivery, including two 25-year studies, one in Europe and the other in the United States. Both the lengthy studies revealed that the use of forceps, Cesarean births, babies in fetal distress, infants stuck in the birth canal or with the umbilical cord wrapped around their neck, all have detrimental effects on the child later in life as well as in the immediacy of the delivery process.

The Birth Process:

"The physiological events of birth are charged with emotional and symbolic power. The circumstances of our birth provide the material from which we create our primary life scripts, which from deep within our minds will exert a gravitational pull on all our thoughts and actions for the rest of our lives" *(Ibid.* p. 78).

- Natural, un-medicated vaginal birth produces babies tending to be self-confident, energetic and trusting of her/his own strength.

- Babies born under anesthesia (80 percent of births) have more difficulty with the bonding process than those born without anesthesia, and feel confused or paralyzed under stress later in life.

- Due to stress, adults who were born from an induced birth tend to feel angrier and more resentful than those who experienced no such interference.

- In adulthood, those delivered with forceps are often defensive to the touch, with anxieties about being stroked, cuddled, or held. Under stress they tend to suffer with headaches, shoulder and neck pain.

15

- Cesarean birth babies are moved by "cuddle hunger." They are prone to be hypersensitive about issues of separation and anxiety.

- Cesarean birth babies, who experience some contractions, sense that they are unable to complete or succeed at a task.

- Babies born with the umbilical cord wrapped around their neck fear suffocation and often end up with psychosomatic illness involving neck and/or vocal cords.

- Breech babies (5 percent of deliveries) are, generally speaking, more headstrong, determined, and stubborn than others.

- The average crying time for a baby who experienced birth trauma is two to six hours per day. The child born without trauma cries to communicate a need and the average time is 20 minutes per day.

"Some studies link especially difficult or traumatic births to drug abuse, violence and even suicide. Birth records of 52 suicide victims (1957-1967) were compared to 104 controls and it was found that records showed poor prenatal care, mothers chronically ill during pregnancy and respiratory difficulty occurred for at least 1 hour after birth." Ibid. p. 81

Some people find it very difficult to believe that what took place in the womb experience affects who we are today. The question that we would ask in response to such an opinion would be this: How would a child's physical development be impacted by what transpires in the womb, but not his or her emotional or psychological development? You see, the mind is developing in the womb too, and what impacts mother, impacts baby's brain and mind as well. God was right all along, and we just didn't understand it. "The sins of the fathers are transferred to the third and fourth generation" (see Ex. 20: 5).

Summing up:

There is a reason that we both (Ron and Nancy) had such an immediate and strong attraction for each other. It was the emptiness we both experienced very early in life from the parent of the opposite sex. This, in fact, was while we were in our mothers' wombs and for a lengthy time beginning right after our births.

Subconsciously, Ron was looking for a mother figure who would provide for him the affection and adoration he missed throughout his infancy and early childhood, and Nancy was endeavoring to fill the hole in her heart left by first, an absent father, and then a controlling father.

The reason for the *instantaneous* attraction is that Ron had just spent several years in prison and was no doubt quite needy of female companionship. His strong attraction for Nancy specifically was because she reminded him of his sister who was nine years old when he was born and who provided most of his care in his early years. Men tend to be attracted to women who remind them of their mother-figures.

Nancy was attracted by two things: Ron's appearance and his attitude. For years she had dreamed of marrying a tall, blond-haired fellow, and he fit that bill. She also dreamed of marrying a minister, and in the first few minutes after they met he had said that he planned to attend college to become a minister. Nancy was of the "helping" type, and she would fit right in to help put him through college.

"Our wounds (say Ron and Nancy), similar but not identical, were the magnets that initially drew us to each other. While, at the time, we honestly believed that our hearts were connecting, the truth is that the wounds we'd each experienced, stored in our minds and hearts, as well as the resulting effects of them in our lives, were reaching each other's heart."

The human heart—which for most people has the capability of reaching out four and-a-half feet, and for some people up to ten—was sensing in the other the need for understanding and compassion. Ron's need for a mother figure and Nancy's for a father figure encountered each other in those first moments of introduction, and they honestly felt that they had just met the partner of their dreams.

"In reality, we had just met another who could fill the holes, the void left from our childhood emptiness."

Birth and early childhood experiences set up the way that we as teens and adults will live later in life. The in-womb experience, far from what many have "always" thought, is primary to the physical, emotional, and spiritual relationships we will feel as our lives progress. Even the actual birth process, the trauma we may have endured during that critical period of time may be a key to our feelings, thoughts, attitudes, and behaviors today.

We are attracted to those whose level of trauma or abuse experienced is quite equal to our own. While the abuse may not be identical or perpetrated upon us by those in the same relationship to us as those who abused our mates, still we look for someone who is at the same level of emotional maturity or health as we are. However, one cannot point a finger at a partner and say that, he /she "is the one to blame for all the problems in our relationship now." That statement would not be true in any sense of the word.

"We (Ron and Nancy) had both experienced wounds in childhood. Some were worse than others, and some had been blanketed with a sense of tenderness and affection that covered the pain hidden beneath. When we met and became acquainted, we were drawn magnetically to each other because of our wounds and the sense that the other could heal them. But how would it be possible for our two hearts to unite? How could we actually feel the pain of the other and have the necessary "tools" to repair our partner's damage? In actuality, neither of us knew the details of the other's wounds, and it was only when those details were finally exposed, *and we each began our own personal healing,* that our hearts could actually become one as the Bible has promised: 'and they will become one flesh'" (Gen. 2: 24).

Questions to Answer and Share with your Partner

1. Before I read this chapter, I thought that the reason I was attracted to my partner was:

2. What I have heard, or what I recall about my parents' marriage is:

3. I believe that some of the characteristics that I inherited from my predecessors are:

CHAPTER TWO

Attachments

Both Keith and Dawn were first-born children in their family of origin. Being a first-born usually makes the child quite responsible, both in childhood and in later adult years. As a first-born grows up, he or she tends to take responsibility for younger siblings. First-borns easily learn the art of being "in charge," and are quite adept at bossing others around.

They met at a gas station when Dawn was just out of high school. She loved Keith's energetic cuteness and his blond wavy hair, and even though he was not talkative she stopped by the station every day for a small amount of gas just to see him. He was extremely shy, and it took several visits before they actually had a conversation. A long, holiday weekend was upcoming and Dawn found enough courage to ask, "If you're off work, do you want to do something?" Date one led to date two and on and on.

Before we continue with Keith and Dawn's story, let's interject a bit of science here that will be helpful in your understanding of yourself and your mate, and how individuals become who they are.

There is a formula which seems to sum up very well just how we as human beings develop into who we are and what we are like. It is as follows:

Chromosomes + Circumstances + Choices = Character

Let's define these words.

Chromosomes: the linear or circular DNA-containing bodies of organisms that contain most or all of the genes of an individual. It is an organized structure of coiled DNA found in cells.

Circumstances: conditions, facts, or events that accompany, condition, or determine another; an accessory fact or detail.

Choices: alternatives or options

Character: the sum total of our thoughts and feelings; who we really are rather than the façade we often wear.

DNA: coiled, long-term storage of information (blueprint, recipe or code)

GENE: Holds the information to build and maintain cells and pass genetic traits, both physical and emotional, to the offspring

Science tells us that we carry at least four generations of genes; so does the Bible (Deut. 5: 6-21). Our parents, our grandparents on both sides of the family, our great- grandparents, and our great-great grandparents have all contributed to who we are. That adds up to you carrying thirty (30) others in your body and mind beside yourself! What an overload of history.

Medical science has always thought that genes could not be changed, but now a new picture is being painted

Keith was born not long after his parents married. His father, a widower, already had three nearly grow children. They lived only a short time in the newly established home of Keith's parents before leaving to establish their separate lives. In the years after Keith's birth four more children were born into the household. Keith remembers that when his father was alive there was considerable arguing and tension in his home. As Keith recalls, his father was an "out of the box" kind of a guy, who lived life largely, laughed loudly, and fought loudly too! But right after the birth of the last child, Keith's father died of a massive heart attack. Suddenly Keith's mom was a widow—with five children to rear alone.

Even though Keith was "put in charge of the family" at age 10, he was seldom at home. His grandparents lived close by and Keith often found "work" to do at their house. He loved the quiet, accepting atmosphere over at Grandma and Grandpa's. He became a hard worker, who rated his success according to the amount of money he was able to make. Still his role as "head of the house" made him a "father figure" to his siblings, and unfortunately a surrogate husband-type to his mother. He was his mother's chosen, her first-born son, and the apple of her eye. While Keith did not have the same strong the emotional attachment to her as she did for him—in fact it was not strong at all— his sense of responsibility was very strong, and he faithfully attended to her needs.

Dawn was born to a couple from dubious backgrounds and it seemed that no one in her family was particularly attached to another. Early on in life she learned the meaning of loss and sadness.

Dawn's mother, Polly, was also an only child, born to a couple who immigrated to the United States from their birth country, leaving Polly in the charge of another family member. This significant move was, in part, an attempt to fix their marriage by "starting over." Polly remained with this family member for several years—until it was convenient for her parents to bring her to America. The relationship Polly had with them afterward was complicated, in that while she loved them to a degree, she carried resentment for their abandoning of her.

Dawn's father was raised almost as a vagabond, going from one foster home to another during his childhood and early adolescence, and finally going out on his own in his teen years. Certainly he carried a history of rejection and poor connections, with the accompanying pain. As a result, he became an alcoholic. His wounds greatly diminished his sense of worth and value, and he married a woman (Polly) who would be controlling and disagreeable, thus exacerbating his view of himself and his drinking habit.

They lived together for several years, but were never truly content or happy. During that time they had three children—Dawn, a son, and a daughter. Between the second and third child Dawn's dad left for a while, then returned. Shortly after the birth of Dawn's sister he left for good. The separation was finalized with a divorce. This was Dawn's first loss of a male figure.

After her parents' divorce, Dawn, her mother, and siblings went to live with her grandparents. While Dawn remembered her father, her little sister did not. Life with her grandparents went well until Grandfather's death, which again brought the grief and experience of loss. Polly seemed to live above the everyday experiences of life, for the most part allowing "Nana" the care of her children while she worked outside the home for the needed income. When her son was 12 years old, Dawn's mother sent him to live with his father and his new wife. "I don't want him. He is out of control and won't listen to me," she told Dawn's father. Herein was loss number three for Dawn. All the men in her life seemed to disappear.

In this chapter we will look at **Styles of Attachment**. Every person has one, and it is developed in the first two years of life *from these necessary factors*:

1.   Breastfeeding with the release of oxytocin (the love hormone) and prolactin (assists oxytocin in breast milk production) and the hearing of mother's familiar heartbeat and sight of her expressive face.

2.   Observation of the mother's face. This produces increased levels of the neuropeptide Corticotropin-releasing factor (CRF) that stimulates the pituitary to produce endorphins (feel good hormones),

3.   Time and attention given to the child,

4.   Quick responses to cries of need,

5.   The relationship between mother and father.

The desperation for parents of the opposite sex brought both Keith and Dawn together. A pregnancy outside of marriage caused them to marry. Shortly after the wedding it became obvious that Keith's focus was to make money to support his wife, while still helping his mother financially. What Dawn had seen at that gas station before marriage, continued—along with his silence—after they were married. Long hours apart left Dawn lonely and needy. Baby number one came along, and with him extra financial responsibilities that kept Keith away from home even longer and longer hours. Dawn, who also was working outside the home, began a nonsexual relationship with a guy at work who talked to her, gave her attention, and made her feel important. Keith just kept working. Once the "emotional affair" was uncovered and subsequently made known to the family, Dawn's mother was still non-supportive. For whatever reason, when a second son was born, he was not treated equally to the firstborn.

With time, Keith's suspicions about Dawn grew larger. He could not get beyond her emotional affair, and he drifted further from Dawn both emotionally and physically. His resentment and sense of rejection had escalated until their marriage was about to end. Then Keith heard that there might be hope for them from a pastoral couple who lived nearby.

While there were several issues complicating their relationship, the main issues had been set up in their character forming years (from conception to the seventh year of life). Both Dawn and Keith had learned to not attach to people "close to them" for fear of loss or disappointment. Both their styles of attachment, created in the first two years of life, were "avoidant." Here were two people, longing to be loved and accepted, but without the know-how and nor the ability to love and accept each other.

POINTS TO CONSIDER:

Keith:
1. A firstborn: responsible and lonely
2. Loss of father (his model) at age 10
3. Quiet and introverted
4. Became his mother's surrogate husband (feeling of duty toward her, which she encouraged)
5. Focus was on providing and financial success
6. Conditional acceptance from Mother, based on his behavior

Dawn:
1. A First-born, responsible daughter
2. Experienced male loss three times in childhood—father, grandfather, brother
3. Quiet and introverted
4. Ignored by her mother, abandoned by father
5. Family was unaffectionate.
6. Mother preoccupied with work and her own pursuits; resentment toward Dawn's father

WHY? WHAT CAN BE LEARNED?

Principle 1: The way we, as human beings, will attach to others in *all* of our relationships for the rest of our lives, is determined in the womb experience and during the first two years of life.

According to experts in the field of prenatal influence and early child development, the relationship that a child's parents have with each other strongly influences the child in the womb and in their first two years.

Hearing, seeing, sensing, or feeling the atmosphere—all that impacts the child's emerging ability to emotionally attach for the rest of the child's life.

The above statement may be very hard to accept because for years we've heard that infants and small children know and remember nothing. But the truth is that their brains are like giant sponges, constantly soaking in information and feelings from the outside world. They learn by observing the interactions between their parents or others with whom they live. The events that take place around them become the cornerstones of their lives, the bricks upon which they build their thought processes and behaviors.

Dr. Thomas Verny, an expert in the field of prenatal influence and experiences, states: "*We now know that the unborn child is an aware, reacting human being who from the sixth month on (and perhaps even earlier) leads an active emotional life.*" In his book, *The Secret Life of the Unborn Child*, he states that the emotional life of the fetus begins at four months gestation. Along with this startling finding, the following discoveries have also been made:

- "The fetus can see, hear, experience, taste and, on a primitive level, even learn *in utero* [that is – in the uterus – before birth]. Most importantly, he can *feel* – not with an adult's sophistication, but feel nonetheless."

- "A corollary to this discovery is that what a child feels and perceives, begins shaping his attitudes and expectations about himself. Whether he ultimately sees himself and, hence, acts as a happy or sad, aggressive or meek, secure or anxiety ridden person depends, in part, on the messages he gets about himself in the womb."

- "The chief source of shaping those messages is the child's mother. *This does not mean that every fleeting worry, doubt or anxiety a woman has rebounds on her child.* What matters are deep, persistent *patterns* of feeling. Chronic anxiety or a wrenching ambivalence about motherhood can leave a deep scar on an unborn child's personality. On the other hand, such life-enhancing emotions as joy, elation and anticipation can contribute significantly to the emotional development of a healthy child."

- "New research is also beginning to focus on the father's feelings. Until recently his emotions were disregarded. Our latest studies indicate that this view is dangerously wrong. **They show that**

how a man feels about his wife and unborn child is one of the single most important factors in determining the success of a pregnancy" (*The Secret Life on the Unborn Child,* pp. 12, 13, bold type supplied).

In a study performed by Dr. Dennis Stott with more than 1,300 children and their families, he estimates that a woman locked into a stormy marriage runs a 237 percent risk of bearing a psychologically or physically damaged child compared to a woman in a secure, nurturing relationship. His study found that unhappy marriages produced babies who were five times more fearful and jumpy than the offspring of happy relationships. These babies continued to be plagued by problems well into childhood. At age four or five, Dr. Stott found them to be undersized, timid, and emotionally dependent on their mothers to an inordinate degree. He states:

"The womb is the child's first world. How he experiences it—as friendly or hostile—does create personality and character predispositions. The womb, in a very real sense, establishes the child's expectations. If it has been a warm, loving environment, the child is likely to expect the outside world to be the same. This produces a predisposition to trust, openness, extroversion, and self-confidence. The world will be his oyster, just as the womb has been. If that environment has been hostile, the child will anticipate that this new world will be equally uninviting. He will be predisposed to suspiciousness, distrust, and introversion. Relating to others will be hard, and so will self-assertion. Life will be more difficult for him than for a child who had a great womb experience" (*Ibid.,* p. 50).

As we learned in Chapter 1, this is not an unchangeable life sentence. All of this can be changed! You are fixable.

That is what recovery done through the power of God is all about!

Principle 2: There are four styles of attachment. We develop our own style by the end of the second year of life, based on interactions with parents or primary caregivers.

Attachment is something that happens *in the child* as a consequence of repeated interactions with the parent blended with internal forces. Studies have shown that the attachment process is a significant factor in healthy development.

We develop an attachment style based on the interactions between ourselves as infants and our mothers, who have a slightly more powerful influence than do fathers.

Dr. John Bowlby, the famous British psychologist who studied children and the effect of detachment or lack of connecting in childhood upon the child, and is the primary authority on attachment, concludes that stable and reliant personality is built on the foundation of the child having absolute accessibility to and support from his or her attachment figures.

Perhaps stating it more simply, attachment is the ability to be certain, with no question in mind, that the child can always get to his or her parents and they will welcome them with open arms. This is the foundation of a secure, autonomous (able to stand on one's own two feet) character and qualities in later life.

Because the brain is built for survival of itself and of the body, it has a tendency to idealize—to put on a pedestal—parents who were NOT what the child needed. The child so desperately wants and needs an intimate relationship with the parent, that it can find some good quality or ability that a parent has, capitalize on that, place the parent on a pedestal and worship even the dysfunction!

Earliest relationships literally shape the chemical processes in the brain responsible for:

- Controlling impulses.

- Calming strong emotions.

- Developing memories of early family life.

When children have been through separation, through the **Protest phase** when they cry and scream for parents to return, through the **Despair Phase**, when they are withdrawn, listless, and in mourning, and through the **Detachment Phase**, when they basically give up on the relationship being reestablished, they develop:

1. **The ability to wall off their emotions.**

2. **The ability to eliminate negative feelings about separation.**

3. **A replacement defense:**

   - A calloused self

   - A system of replacing things for relationships

   - The ability to bury their need for trust, intimacy, and closeness

   - A refusal to reach out to anyone for emotional comfort

   - A reliance on self and the material things they came to love

Let's look at the **Style of Attachment** that Keith and Dawn developed in early childhood. These styles last a lifetime without intervention for repairing wounds.

Keith, the Avoidant: *"We never fought, because we never talked."*
AVOIDANTS:

- Make sure that they remain self-sufficient and in control
- Avoid intense emotions
- Dodge conversations that may elicit strong emotions or emotional closeness
- Usually marry anxiously attached people who search for closeness, affirmation, and cling
- Respond to their anxious partner by remaining emotionally contained and aloof, and then try to regulate their partner's emotional level
- Attitude is: *Nearness means getting disappointed and hurt. It's best to stay disconnected, distant, and disengaged from emotional involvement. Loneliness is better than agony.*

In the list of Avoidant behaviors, which ones do you think apply to you?

Dawn, the Ambivalent: Had strong but ambivalent (hesitant and undecided) emotions.

The vacillating emotion corrodes the sense of self and clouds the belief that they have the ability to be loved.

AMBIVALENTS:

- Play the part of the servant, the pleaser, the performer.
- Cling desperately to the partner, regardless of his/her abusive behaviors.
- Do not develop enough confidence to have a career or accomplishments "on their own".

- If being a wife or husband has been taught/modeled to them in childhood, they take care of their partners, meeting all their needs and then some, to prevent them from leaving or dying.

- Uses whichever "dependent" style is his/hers to "keep the mate".

- Builds up internal resentments because "of all the work I do to keep him/her happy!"

- Becomes increasingly more dependent due to multiple illnesses.

In the list of Ambivalent behaviors, which ones do you think apply to you?

In Keith's and Dawn's story, add to this the intimacy ingredient that should be in marriage. "In-to-me-see" conversation would not take place, because Keith (the protected self) would refuse to share his thoughts and feelings, perhaps he would actually deny having feelings. Dawn (the fearful self) would be afraid of sharing how she really felt because she would be afraid of pushing Keith further away than he already was.

The <u>tendency of the avoidant is to push others away</u> by making hurtful comments and painful put-downs. <u>The ambivalent remains silent for fear of being rejected</u> or abused.

There is another aspect of intimacy to consider: sexuality. In this kind of marriage, who would initiate sexual intimacy? Would it be the one who clings and is fearful, or would it be the one who runs away, expecting that the fearful one will chase?

Sex between married couples is an expression of their oneness, their intimacy. If the oneness is absent, what happens to their sex life? Perhaps it becomes purely functional rather than emotional and enjoyable for both. How long can that last? If either or both had experienced sexual wounds in childhood or adolescence, sexuality would be an added complication. Resolving this complication in a marriage would require professional psychological intervention and intimate communication.

Can you see how it would be possible for a couple who have this combination, to live in misery? One clings and the other runs or pushes the partner away with verbal barbs. It makes you wonder if they could ever get it together, doesn't it. The answer to turning this and any other troubled marriage into a great one is:

- to be willing to work at processing through the **reasons** why each of you developed the style that you possess,

- to work at the undoing of the emotions attached to your childhood memories of wounds received, and

- to learn the techniques that will enhance your oneness.

This will shift your marriage from one of misery to one of awareness of self and your mate, and on to acceptance of yourself and of each other.

Principle 3: There are two other Attachment Styles to review.

The third dysfunctional type is called **Disorganized—the Shattered Self.** It is developed in a home where:

- Psychological abuse

- Emotional neglect

- Physical abuse+

- Sexual abuse (incest and/or molestation)

- Severe marital conflict or

- Addictive behaviors are present.

People with the Disorganized Attachment Style feel trapped in a chaotic world, one of rapidly shifting emotions, impulsive behaviors, and muddled relationships.

The Disorganized suffer with:

1. **Identity problems:** They have trouble learning from past experiences and are unable to consider future consequences.

2. **Emotional Storms:** They have inappropriate fits of rage and full-blown panic attacks. They agonize with chronic feelings of depression and experience little pleasure in daily life. They experience unpredictable flashbacks with overwhelming emotion.

3. **Physical Arousal:** They are on edge, a state of physical alertness in which the body is ready to either flee or fight.

4. **Identification with the Aggressor**: They take the blame for the aggression received as a child and idolize the real aggressor—especially if the aggressor was a parent.

5. **Faulty Assumptions**: "The reason I'm being hurt is that there's something wrong with me." Obsessive/compulsive behaviors make them think they are controlling their situation.

6. **Distressed Relationships**: Their lack of trust, fear of abandonment, fear of intimacy and, altered sexuality dooms their relationships. They alternate between control freak and doormat, and seem determined to keep repeating the trauma of the past.

In the list of Disorganized behaviors, which ones do you think apply to you?

Secure Attachment: This is the style that everyone would love to have and few do. It would be necessary to grow up in a home where dysfunction is basically absent, and where peace and harmony reigns. How many families can boast that?

Those who are securely attached:

- Are confident about "Who I am."
- Don't feel the pressure to perform.
- Relate to others genuinely and confidently (no hidden agendas).
- Don't take criticism personally.
- Respect the feelings of others—are not threatened by them.
- They know how to negotiate conflict.
- Skilled at communicating feelings and opinions without running rough-shod over others.
- Have a basic trust in others.
- Know how to express anger in a healthy non-threatening manner. The healthy expression of anger can actually be a healing experience.

Do you have any behaviors of the Securely attached?

It is possible, with help and work done, to move from a dysfunctional style to a secure attachment with a mate. Doing so would be a major contributor to marital success and happiness.

Have you found your Attachment Style? If you aren't sure, consider processing through the first segment of the recovery program called *The Journey*. It will help you to identify your style and process through the resulting behaviors. The process itself will assist you to move toward secure attachment. Look for the information about an **Inventory** which identifies your attachment style at the end of the book.

How did the attachment styles of Keith and Dawn affect them and their marriage?

For several years after the birth of their second son, Keith and Dawn lived like married singles. He worked, and worked, and then worked some more. She stayed home with the children, even after they started in school. She baked and cooked and did what she could to create a "family," but had difficulty because Keith was gone from home at work so much of the time. Keith continued to hold onto sadness and resentment because of the old "affair," while Dawn's resentment escalated because of what she felt was an empty relationship. Meanwhile, Keith continued to be a financial support to his mother, paying her mortgage payment each month. Not surprisingly, the relationship between Dawn and Keith's mother did not improve. As far as Keith's mother was concerned, he "could've done better in choosing a wife." She accused Dawn of being a "poor" mother.

Feeling rejected, unimportant, and valueless, Dawn decided that she could not continue in their relationship. The marriage was over, as far as she was concerned. She began to pack her bags, intending to leave Keith and the boys. At that, Keith went into crisis and panic. This is when he approached the pastor and his wife who lived just down the street and begged for immediate help. Help began the next day at their home as Dawn agreed to wait one week before she departed.

Keith shared with the pastor, "We have never fought, but that is because we never talked!"

By the end of that week, they had begun to see some of the ingredients that had thwarted their happiness, and resolved to make needed changes. They jumped into the process with both feet, so to speak, attending weekend seminars on marriage and even becoming a support couple at those weekends. Their marriage began to improve, and today, 30 years later, they are still together, still learning. Keith's tendency is to be silent, to keep things to himself, to not share the nitty-gritty of everyday life with Dawn, and Dawn tends to build girlfriend relationships outside the home for the connection she needs. Periodically it will dawn on them what they are doing and they will come together, take a trip together, or just spend a day having fun.

They have endured a life tragedy that has caused many a couple to end their marriage— the death of their eldest son. It was a devastating loss to the entire family to lose a fair-haired son who, at age 19 seemed destined for life success. Usually in such a tragedy, husband and wife blame each other, resentment builds, and marriage finally ends. But Keith and Dawn weathered that storm and the subsequent loss of their financial fortune, and then the loss of their health, necessitating a move across country to a drier climate.

Do they still have hurdles that have not been completely overcome? Of course, but a willingness on their part to "stay in the conversation," to learn, to apply what they learn to themselves, to resolve what stands in their way of complete happiness, will insure their continued improvement. They still battle the temptation to be emotionally distant—the lesson they learned in childhood. However, they have in their toolbox, the tools needed for intimate and satisfying conversation. They just need to remember to use them.

As Keith and Dawn continue to work at self-understanding and intimate communication with one another their hearts will continue in the process of becoming one. Their connection will advance to a more complete heart to heart connection, with each knowing themselves and each other well. Discordant notes will become harmonious as their two hearts connect and beat as one.

IN SUMMARY:

It is during the first two years of life that we develop and "settle on" our Style of Attachment. The atmosphere in our homes and the relationships with parents or primary caregivers, especially watching Mother and Father interact with each other, are the ingredients that combine to form the way we will attach to our parents and to others as we get older. The attachment style we develop in those early months and years will impact many aspects of our lives, as we saw in the story of Keith and Dawn. There are even aspects of life, not covered in their story, that are influenced by that initial unconscious decision to be Avoidant, Ambivalent, Disorganized, or Secure.

So, when Keith and Dawn met, was it the connection of two hearts, or was it the connection of two needy souls? Having read their story, you would no doubt agree that it wasn't their hearts that connected, but their desperate needs. Dawn needed a father, and in Keith she saw a cute, pleasant, hard-working provider. Perhaps he would be the one to fill the giant hole in her heart where her father should have been throughout childhood and adolescence. Keith saw an attractive blond, but in truth was no doubt attracted by the repeated visits to his gas station, giving him the message that she accepted and admired and most of all respected him. Their earliest unmet needs had set up their later needs, and they reacted to the emptiness they felt, feeling that they could be filled by each other.

Is it possible to improve one's own ability to attach?

Absolutely!

What does it require? A look at history, at our earliest relationships, at the specific influences we felt when we were young and in later childhood and adolescence. The devastating early hurtful experiences, while they aren't erased from the brain designed to remember, can be minimized in the process of recovery. When we address the truth about our experiences, deal with those who hurt us, regardless of where they are or even if they are still alive, we remove the negative emotional charge from the memories, and are able to let bitterness and resentment go—as the Bible tells us to do (Eph. 4:30, 31).

Questions for you to answer and share

1. What do you know about your parent's upbringing and the circumstances of their childhoods until about age 13?

2. On a scale of 1 to 10, what number would you assign to the happiness of your parents' marriage when you were a child?

   Miserable - 1 2 3 4 5 6 7 8 9 10 - Very Happy

3. What significant losses do you recall from your childhood years?

4. With whom were you most attached during childhood?

CHAPTER THREE

Anger and Mashed Potatoes

God created all of us with an inborn need to be loved and wanted and to belong to someone. Some parents, due to their own inability to attach to their parents when they were children, have difficulty bonding with their own unborn or newly born infants. If parents bond to their child while he or she is still in the womb and in the extremely sensitive period immediately after birth (the first four hours) as well as during the first two years of life, the child will attach in a healthy manner to the parent. This attachment is exactly what each human being should have had in their beginnings, albeit, few are thus blessed.

All of her life, Doris longed to belong, just like everyone else who was ever born, but that had never been her experience. How difficult it was for her to be the youngest girl of ten children, to be ignored and discounted or tormented by her older siblings. Actually, she hardly knew them at all, because so many were years older than her. She just knew their scorn, rejection, and sometimes outright abuse.

The atmosphere in her house was toxic! The family diet consisted of noodles and more noodles, soup, beans, and one chicken on Sundays to feed them all. They lived in a tiny, tarpaper-covered shack by the river, and their dark, damp basement was the scariest place in the house.

Dad was an uneducated and definitely unsophisticated alcoholic. He worked for meager wages, and having ten children to feed must have caused him considerable angst. His anger was up front most of the time,

36

and demeaning insults and four-letter expletives were commonplace. Mother worked hard to care for her kids as best she could, but most of the time was emotionally distant. Hugging and cuddling were nonexistent. Truth is, Mother had never really experienced it in her beginnings, and Dad hadn't either. They couldn't give out what they never had—their own childhood experiences had been nightmarish, at best.

Dad often beat his wife, and if it wasn't his wife he was abusing, it was one or more of the kids. Sometimes after Mom had been beaten, she would lock herself in her bedroom for days.

Perhaps following Mom's example in a twisted way, the older sisters would lock Doris in the shed, and leave her unattended for hours or days. The worst was when Dad, or one of her brothers, pinned her down and violated her sexually. Her tiny rollaway bed would often be wet in the mornings, (bedwetting is common in children who have been, or are being sexually abused). When that happened she'd be tossed across the wet bed, it would be folded around her then carried out into the snow for several hours.

How she longed to feel loved, just once.

Her only place of comfort was down the street at a church where she would go and "camp" under a pew. There she created a make-belief family and lived a fantasy life with love and attention she created herself.

You read this and say to yourself, why would you write such a horrible, painful tale? Very few people have endured that kind of rejection. Maybe that's true, but to a greater or lesser degree, all of us have known the sting of not being invited, not being chosen, or of being ignored.

Studies for 47 years by Dr. Ronald Rohner of the University of Connecticut have discovered that the *four criteria people use to identify rejection in their life are:*

• Warmth and Affection?

• Hostility and Aggression?

• Neglect and Ignoring?

• Undifferentiated (can't quite put your finger on it but you feel it)?

Not all stories are so dramatic or devastating, but any rejection is painful nonetheless.

And the reason we tell Doris's story? We share it because it is a powerful testimony to the redeeming love of God, who reached down to this broken life, gave her a companion, and began the slow process toward healing.

So what about her partner, her husband? Dave was the first-born child of a very young mother, whose husband was in the military. Her pregnancy and delivery were without the support of her husband, and for the first few years of his life Dave had only a teenage mother as his model, his caretaker.

When Dad came home, several other children soon came along. Mom and Dad were strict religionists, and Dave was made to tow the line. Very quickly, he learned that his worth and value was tied to the work he could perform, and the excellence with which he did it. He was criticized extensively by his father, and made to work long hours for little benefit. Pats on the back were non-existent. He became an extreme perfectionist (as is often the case when a child is raised with criticism).

When Dave reached high school he was sent off to a religious boarding school for his education. There he encountered more restriction and fanaticism. When he graduated he returned to his parents and to the farm that his father managed. It was in that town that he and Doris met.

Living in poor conditions—many years without indoor plumbing and little in the way of luxury or material possessions—he became a very hard worker on the farm. Actually his pay was so meager, that when he and Doris married, they had to live there on the farm in a shack with no running water until, between his wages and a small income from Doris' job, they were able to rent a small apartment.

Dave was older than Doris, quiet and reserved, and looked like the exact, stable influence she needed. Doris was a very bright young woman, and Dave an intelligent young man. Both had been excellent students. It seemed theirs was a match made in heaven, and they quickly determined to marry. Unfortunately, it would be years before each shared the details of the childhood abuse they had suffered. Both were very hard workers, so it was no surprise to learn that Doris worked until the last minute the evening of her wedding. After work she went home, put on her wedding dress, and she and Dave went to the preacher's home where their ceremony was performed.

And then the "fun" began!

On to their Honeymoon Hotel. Doris took her shower, got her PJ's on, and hopped into one of the room's *twin* beds. Dave took his shower, donned his PJ's and then stood in the room trying to decide which bed to get into. He chose the other bed. Doris was devastated. Here her history of violent rejection in her family of origin was again being played out, and this time by the man she loved. How could this be? Finally, about half an hour later, as she lay on her pillow in a puddle of tears, Dave asked if she thought he should get in bed with her.

Their early marriage was replete with incidents they do not want to remember today! Doris, an excellent cook, would prepare a meal, and Dave would turn up his nose at what she presented. In subsequent years they peeled mashed potatoes—and other foods—off the ceiling, where angry and feeling rejected, Doris had thrown his uneaten supper.

Rejection piled upon rejection was just too much for her, and every time it raised its ugly head, which was on a regular basis, trouble would follow. While they really loved each other, Doris could never seem to get it "right" for her perfectionist husband. The harder she tried to please him, the more he criticized. Wonder where he learned to do that? At work (Doris often worked alongside Dave), he criticized Doris, and at home he was silent.

The children that came along were somewhat of a distraction to their painful relationship. Doris mothered the kids and Dave spent a lot of time at work. Doris made the "heavy" decisions and Dave let her, all the while criticizing her choices. Doris worked in their home, cared for their children, and worked alongside Dave in his work—being judged and criticized as she did. Then Doris would retreat into the horror of her continued rejection and Dave would retreat into his work. Finally in self-defense, Doris began criticizing Dave. That definitely did not improve their relationship! It seemed that the way they could have peace was to just keep working hard, and avoid anything even slightly emotional.

Would they ever find enjoyment in each other? Would life ever be simple enough for them to face the rejection that divided and re-wounded them both every single day of their lives? Would it be possible to ever find some peace and contentment?

And then something happened. It was at church that the frightening, terrifying opportunity of a lifetime was announced—an upcoming seminar. It took a lot of convincing by the pastor's wife, but finally Doris agreed to attend. Here began her metamorphosis, her slow but sure, deliberate change. However, Dave would have nothing to do with it! He resented religion in the first place, and how could such a perfectionist (as himself) admit to having imperfections or issues? Regardless of the fact that the seminar was not about religion, but about wounds and their effect on a life, Dave couldn't handle even the idea of it. And anyway, work was always a good excuse.

But . . .

When the person to whom you are closest begins to change, then *you* have to change too or watch your relationship become more and more distant. Slowly, as your partner begins to behave differently, you have to begin to look at yourself. At first it may be an affront to you as your partner begins to display hope, goodness, and positive change. After all, it makes your own darkness seem all the more dismal. But eventually as things get better, you begin to see "light at the end of the tunnel."

Does this mean that Doris changed overnight? Absolutely not! However, as her interests changed, as she built new friendships, as Dave saw her reading, studying her Bible (and there were no more mashed potatoes flung at the ceiling), he began to show a bit more interest in recovery. Don't get the idea that he jumped in with both feet, but he did attend a seminar, and at least started the recovery process. Does he like to talk about his history? Does he like to admit his issues? Not really, but there's hope even there. God will do whatever is necessary to get our attention, to point us to a better way, to call us to Him.

Near death experiences have a way of getting our attention too, and Dave has been there, done that, at a comparatively young age. His willingness to speak, to share has improved. He still is a perfectionist, and to a degree, that's admirable, especially when it relates to his detailed work. His life has changed. His illnesses have seen to that, but so has his marriage. His criticizing of Doris has diminished considerably, and Doris no longer feels that she must run away from friends because she thinks they are rejecting her. They have weathered the storm and come out on the other side of it, scarred but healing.

Lessons Doris learned in childhood:

1. <u>That she was not wanted, and therefore must be seriously flawed.</u> Children take responsibility for whatever they see, hear, or experience. She felt that the dysfunction in her family of origin must be her fault!

2. <u>Trust no one!</u> When those who should have been the closest to you (parents and siblings) reject you, then everyone else will too.

3. <u>My lot in life is to be used and abused.</u> If that is your deduction from what you've experienced, then your tendency is to expect and even promote this in later life.

4. <u>When the going gets rough, EXPLODE!</u> Mashed potatoes on the ceiling or internal war. Don't speak what you really feel, because that will cause trouble. Exploding lasts only a few moments.

Lessons Dave learned in childhood:

1. <u>Criticism is the way to get what you want.</u> Apparently that's what Dave deducted from his own experience of being criticized. And that helps you to keep people at an emotional distance too, and for an avoidant it's a workable tactic.

2. <u>Perfectionism can help you to avoid being criticized.</u> Actually you'll be admired and affirmed. Of course the problem with perfectionism is that you then expect perfection from everyone else, especially spouses and children.

3. <u>Keep your thoughts and feelings to yourself!</u> If you are quiet, others will never know what you're thinking, which gives them the inability to criticize your thoughts and feelings. You remain in control.

4. <u>Don't feel. Frozen emotions will cause less pain!</u> In actuality however, frozen emotions cause you to "stuff" feelings, causing physical illness and greater emotional pain.

Principle 1:

Rejection: the most devastating of all wounds.

It's a bone-chilling word, rejection. The sound of it conjures up memories of slights received and of tears shed. With it comes the poor self-worth that results from the wound. "There must be something wrong with me. What have I done or said to be cast off like yesterday's underwear?"

Most of the responses to rejection are self-destructive. The torture of keeping a mental list of abuses received only piles up resentment and bitterness with the list. Eventually, an explosion of catastrophic dimensions will occur—the fallout landing on either oneself or on those with whom a victim is in close relationship, or maybe even on the ceiling! Retaining slights or purposeful rejections builds a set of gray, cloudy glasses worn every day by the victim and used to predict reactions from all they meet.

If in your character-forming years you felt like you did not belong to your family and friends, or if you currently find yourself feeling like a fifth wheel with acquaintances or even with family, you no doubt are experiencing the results of earlier rejection. The 48 years of study in parental rejection and acceptance, conducted by Dr. Ronald Rohner of the University of Connecticut's Family Studies Department, conclude that if a person *perceives* he is rejected, he has received it (*Handbook for the Study of Parental Acceptance and Rejection*, p.1).

One's perception becomes one's reality. If you find yourself being sensitive to the slights of others, predicting that friends or family will reject you, you are experiencing two of the behaviors and thoughts of those who have been rejected early on in life.

What is Rejection? It is a refusal to accept, to hear, to touch, or to consider important. It is to discard, push aside, or discount, and it is an emotionally charged knowledge that you are not loved and wanted for yourself by one or both parents.

Rejection Produces:

- A feeling that one is not loved, wanted, or accepted for themselves by one or both parents (*real or perceived*).
- A self-defeating feeling of hopelessness arising from damages occurred during prenatal and early childhood years.
- A depressing feeling of not belonging which seems to pervade every moment and every association of life.
- A prediction of rejection from every relationship, and will cause one to sabotage relationships that appear to be successful, in order to feel "normal." To that person, being rejected is what's normal.
- A blockage from love, and victims are left alone to fend for themselves.
- A silent killing of intimacy.
- A feeling of being unloved and unlovable.
- The need to wear a mask of normalcy.
- The ability to keep our relationships in place, but leaves the heart alone.
- A shut down that blocks receiving and giving.
- A wall, impeding others from entering to offer light or hope.
- A Love of extremes.
- A tendency to have contempt for those who behave differently, making victims cynical and sarcastic. A well-hidden contempt for others. Self-centeredness and low self-worth.

A child who is, or feels that he is criticized regularly, or who lives in a family where criticism is the norm; where other family or friends are criticized, certainly does not feel accepted. When a child feels that they cannot do anything right to please their parents or other family members, he or she gets the idea that they are worthless, just an annoyance, an inconvenience to their parents. That self-devaluation continues for a lifetime, getting increasingly more pronounced with each criticism received. Such self-deprecation makes it hard to receive compliments graciously, even though affirmation is craved. It also creates a difficulty to receive gifts or favors without profuse objection to the one giving to them.

"Rosenberg" Self-Esteem Quiz

Simply complete the self-esteem Quiz questions below. Rate each statement based on how much you agree. Rate your responses as follows:

SD = Strongly Disagree; D = Disagree; A = Agree; SA = Strongly Agree

___ 1. I feel that I'm a person of worth, at least on an equal basis with others.

___ 2. I feel that I have a number of good qualities.

___ 3. All in all, I am inclined to think I'm a failure.

___ 4. I am able to do things as well as most other people.

___ 5. I feel I do not have much to be proud of.

___ 6. I take a positive attitude towards myself.

___ 7. On the whole, I am satisfied with myself.

___ 8. I wish I could have more respect for myself.

___ 9. I certainly feel useless at time.

___ 10. At times I think I'm no good at all.

Scoring Procedures for the Rosenberg Self Esteem Test

Scores are calculated as follows:

For items 1, 2, 4, 6, and 7:
Strongly agree (SA) = 3
Agree (A) = 2
Disagree (D) = 1
Strongly disagree (SA) = 0

For items 3, 5, 8, 9, and 10 (which are reversed in valence):

Strongly agree (SA) = 0
Agree (A) = 1
Disagree (D) = 2
Strongly disagree SD) = 3

The scale ranges from 0 to 30.

A score below 15 suggests low self-esteem; above 15 indicates that self-esteem is healthy and intact. Those with high self-esteem have an unusually positive self-image. Most people with low self-esteem do not have a negative, but rather a neutral self-image.

Picture what it would be when both husband and wife have poor self-worth; giving and receiving love can be next to impossible. Each time the words, "I love you" are said, the hearer disbelieves their partner. They do not say they don't believe in so many words, but their disbelief is definitely observable. The couple remains emotionally distant even while they might be sexually compatible.

Early on in our marriage (Ron and Nancy) we said "I love you" to each other, but Ron thought that Nancy was lying to him and Nancy thought that love from Ron was too good to be true. When one has not received from parents in early childhood, receiving from a partner later in life can be difficult!

It's been said before, but it's worth repeating. Rejected people look for rejection under every rock. They usually find it, but if they don't, they will manufacture rejection in an attempt to keep themselves "right." They will engage in behaviors that are obnoxious enough to get themselves rejected, and will push and push until someone rejects them. Often those behaviors were present in Doris and Dave's marriage, as well as in Ron and Nancy's.

Principle 2:

Trust is a necessary ingredient in marriage, and it is built in the first 18 months of life.

According to Erik Erickson, a well-known psychiatrist, trust is built due to the trustworthiness of parents or primary caregivers to meet the physical and emotional needs of their infant in a timely fashion and with an internal willingness to do so. If we pass successfully through this period of life, we will learn to **trust** that life is basically okay and have confidence in the future. If we fail to experience trust and are constantly frustrated because our needs are not met, we may end up with a deep-seated feeling of worthlessness and a **mistrust** of the world in general. The positive results of accomplishing trust in those first 18 months of life is an internal drive and a sense of hope for the future.

Looking at this lack in Doris and Dave's marriage, it is understandable that trust would be missing in both of them. Trust is the foundation of any solid relationship, and without it, intimacy is elusive. Their conclusion would lean towards, "If you couldn't trust your parents, how can you trust anyone else?"

While they both had a great need to be able to trust, the accomplishment of it came after years of not having it, and then working to build it through a recovery process. If neither could trust the other, and both had not received the love they needed in childhood, they would both have empty hearts that had very little to give to the other, and very little capacity to receive that which they urgently needed. In them would be a drive to find some person or thing that would fill that emptiness. Dave substituted his perfectionist work for heart connection. It was through his work and it's expertly detailed perfection that he connected with anyone, including his wife. It was all he talked about, and that's how he felt safe and in control. Her sense of completion came by doing for others, but underneath it Doris still felt empty and valueless. She often complained that she was not appreciated.

In an excellent book, *Secrets, Lies, Betrayals*, author and professor at Yale University, Maggie Scarf writes:

"... *we often operate in ways that will result in our inner expectations— good or bad—being fulfilled. Our most basic perceptions of the world around us are always being selected and shaped by an internalized blueprint for living that we've developed over time. This 'framework for living' contains the core schemas and dynamic themes—the images of who we are and what we will be—that shape our perceptions of the past and understanding of what lies in the future. At an unconscious level, our personal blueprint underlies the well-known 'self-fulfilling prophecy,' which is to say that what we believe in our hearts—that is, our bodies as well as our minds—about 'the way things are' tends to become true in reality. In some subtle fashion, one that is not usually in reach of conscious awareness, we shape the way the narrative of our life develops*" (p. 20).

Quite a mouthful, wouldn't you say? And it's right on the button! What Scarf is saying, simply stated, is that our memories and the ways in which we have interpreted them, tend to set up the way our life will go in the future. This is the very reason that *Recovery*, the process of eliminating the negative emotional charge from old painful memories so that we can live fully in the present, is designed to help us to predict, expect, and then experience a joy-filled, positive future.

Principle 3: Worth and value is important to attitude and behaviors. If because you lived with abuse you assume that you are worthy of it, you'll tolerate it OR you'll perpetrate it on others in a way similar to how you received it.

The experience in the first seven character-forming years will determine our view of our own worth and value—our self- image. When the Basic Needs of a child have not been met, the child will assume that he or she is the cause of neglect or abuse, thinking, "There must be something wrong with me that I caused my parents behaviors toward me."

The following is a list of the **Basic Needs of a Child**. Make a mental note, or check off those needs that were not well met for you during your childhood.

Unmet Needs: If children *do not*:

- Have mother and father present physically and emotionally
- Receive love and are not allowed to express love to their parents
- Feel accepted (received, heard, included and considered important)
- Hear words of affirmation and encouragement
- Receive support (supply of strength to achieve)
- Get taught age-appropriate truths
- Receive safe and nurturing touch
- Feel that they can trust their parents
- Receive training to govern themselves and make decisions
- Experience active time and caring by the parent(s)
- Feel a sense of security
- Receive wings to fly away at the appropriate age . . .

  they have not had their Basic Needs met, and their sense of personal worth and value is tarnished.

As a parent who's own basic needs were not met in childhood, your tendency would be to swing like the pendulum of a clock. On one hand your tendency would be to *not* meet your child's basic needs if yours were not met well in childhood. On the other hand, you might tend to be very permissive and overly indulgent of your children.

As has already been made clear, both Doris and Dave grew up with painful experiences. Would they become victims or perpetrators? The answer is yes—they would be both!

Dave perpetrated verbal abuse through criticism of Doris' prepared meals and of the way she held a board or helped him with a construction project. He was also gone from the home for long hours and had difficulty connecting emotionally when he was at home. Doris just tried harder and harder for Dave's acceptance, for words of affirmation instead of his impatience and negative put downs, but to no avail. She became an "everything" kind of wife, not only helping Dave with his projects but also perfecting her own crafts and money-making projects. Name it and Doris could do it perfectly, even when working with or for Dave—whether he thought so or not! She also tended to be overly protective of her children.

So how did Doris react to Dave? For a while she took the insults because she thought she deserved them, but eventually the resentment built up and she began to copy the criticism and hand it right back to him. So instead of building each other up, encouraging and uplifting, they shot darts at each other. The merry-go-round of their dysfunction revolved faster and faster on the way to disaster. Was there any hope?

Principle 4: Keeping the stories of your past and your feelings hidden inside you can cause physical and emotional illness.

Have you ever heard the expression, he *died of a broken heart?* You may think it a foolish statement, but in reality, it's not so foolish. Actually scientists and heart specialists have now labeled a new diagnosis: *Broken Heart Syndrome.* This is diagnosed when the patient has no observable heart damage or abnormalities, but has suffered an untoward incident following an emotional upset.

Doctors at John's Hopkins University gave the name to the condition, demonstrated through sophisticated heart tests how it differs from a heart attack, and offered an explanation for what causes it. For a person with what's known as broken heart syndrome, an emotional stress like the death of a loved one can cause a seemingly healthy heart to stop working normally.

Doctors estimate that one to two percent of patients who are diagnosed with a heart attack in the United States are actually suffering broken heart syndrome. It's easy to understand the wrong diagnosis, however, for patients have many of the same symptoms as a heart attack, including chest pains and shortness of breath.

Inside the body, however, broken heart syndrome looks very different from a heart attack. While a heart attack is usually caused by blocked arteries, medical experts believe broken heart syndrome is caused by a surge in adrenaline and other hormones. When patients experience an adrenaline rush in the aftermath of a stressful situation, the heart muscle may be overwhelmed and become temporarily weakened. The left ventricle of the heart takes on a cone-like shape that resembles a Japanese pot used to capture an octopus. That altered shape gives the condition its medical name—*Takotsubo Cardiomyopathy.*

Think about couples who have lived together many years. The husband or wife gets terminal cancer, and the partner cares tenderly for their spouse until death. Then dawns the reality of living alone; grief from the loss seems overwhelming, and the pain of aloneness cannot be endured. Shortly after the death, the living spouse also dies. Prior to the first death, the caretaker's health had not been in question. Death is sudden, and seemingly unexplained.

What is equally fascinating are the results of the ACE study reported in this web article at: http://xnet.kp.org/permanentejournal/winter02/goldtolead.html

The two most important findings are that adverse childhood experiences:

- are vastly more common than recognized or acknowledged, and

- have a powerful relation to adult health a half century later.

  Dr. Maggie Scarf writes on the cover of her book *Secrets, Lies, Betrayals*:

"The body has a unique memory system, in which early trauma and deeply buried feelings become woven into the fabric of our physical being. Certain events can trigger these body memories, which may then manifest themselves symptomatically—as persistent anger, mood swings, headaches, muscle tension and fatigue. The echoes from the past also cause destructive patterns in life and relationships."

She further states, *"The body, through its neurobiological systems, retains some of life's most important experiences"* (*Ibid.*).

Here is a statement we have often used in
our seminars because of its truth:
Whatever is covered up cannot heal.

The wisest choice for complete health is to bring out in the open, into the light of truth, the experiences that frequently or even occasionally, cross our minds. Those childhood (especially early childhood) experiences, the months before we had language but were absorbing like a sponge, (implicit memories) still dictate our world view and often our feelings and behaviors. Memories formed when we did have language ability (explicit) have nearly as much impact as those pre-language, and they cannot be ignored or covered up. They will impact our physical, emotional, relational, and spiritual health or lack thereof. If we do not deal with them (that means that we acknowledge their presence; we examine them) they will deal with us!

Principle 5: Frozen emotions are like ice. Keep them within you long enough and you'll be numb or very ill.

When you put an ice pack on a wound, does it chase away the wound or may it just reduce pain and swelling?

Until fairly recently, people believed that the best treatment for a burn was to slather the affected area with butter. But all that did was to fry the body's tissue in grease! The application of an ice pack helps to remove some of the heat from the burn, thus slowing down the process of tissue destruction. But, does the ice pack heal the burn? Absolutely not!

Dave knows what can happen when one keeps their emotions on ice. A major stroke, another smaller stroke, and four heart attacks—necessitating the use of a defibrillator to bring him back from the brink of death—and several cardiac surgeries were a major wake-up call for Dave. Doris was at his side 24/7 as he suffered and recovered. Has all this changed Dave emotionally? To a degree it has. He has begun to open up a bit more than he had previously, and as he does, his health improves!

We have been told by University of London researchers Dr. Hans Eysenck and R. Grossarth-Maticek that in a 20-year study, it was determined that unmanaged reactions to stress were a more dangerous risk factor for heart disease and cancer than either smoking or high cholesterol.

This study was reported in an article titled "Personality Type, Smoking Habit and Their Interaction as Predictors of Cancer and Coronary Heart Disease," published in *Personality and Individual Differences 9*, (1988): pp. 479-95.

When you keep telling yourself that you do not feel, does that lie remove the cause of your problem? Absolutely not! The problem just is numbed out. Some people use a mind-altering substance such as drugs, alcohol, food, work, or even religion to numb their pain, but does that negate or solve the issue? Sadly, no. It only serves as the blanket to cover up or hide the real hurt.

Thawing out the memories and taking an honest look at them (sometimes with the help of a professional or in a recovery program) and using the tools to undo those pesky negatives from old memories, is what can change your path from one of self-destruction to one of self-*construction*—building a new and hopeful future and an enjoyable marriage.

SUMMING UP

Experiences that you have endured from the womb onward can greatly influence your thoughts and feelings today. In addition, modern scientific studies have proven that unresolved emotional issues from the past can adversely affect both your physical health and your outlook on life.

It is in your earliest months and years that you develop trust, the basic ingredient in all of the relationships you'll have later in life. If you could not develop trust in your parents, your siblings, your grandparents and/or primary caregivers, developing it with friends, perspective marital partners, or with God later in life will happen slowly and with difficulty. Initially the level of intimacy that you can achieve is hampered, but increases as you are willing to work through history, and it is accelerated with the guidance of a recovery program.

Did Doris and Dave have an ethereal heart connection moment when they met, or was it the proverbial "the rocks in his head fit the holes in mine"?

Of course it was the "rocks" and the "holes." Dave, the stable quiet guy was the opposite of the loud, angry, abusive father who had a hard time providing for his family. Doris was the sharp, hardworking, non-intrusive girl who could care for Dave, keep a certain safe distance from him, and would take any criticism he dished out. The h*eart connection* didn't begin arriving until many years later.

These burdensome thoughts, feelings, and behaviors you find occurring in later life are fixable *provided* you are willing to research your past, to discover there the treasure, the key to your current feelings and behaviors. While you may not have recall, there will most assuredly be someone connected to your beginnings who can clue you in and help you to understand the circumstances surrounding your mother's pregnancy and your first months of life.

Questions for You to Answer and Share

1. As you look back over your childhood or adolescent years, can you recall an experience of rejection that has made a negative impact on your life? Write about it and share with your partner.

2. Did you encounter perfectionism or criticism in your childhood or teenage years? Who was the perfectionist and how did that person demand it of you?

3. How do you react when you feel a friend or family member has rejected or betrayed you?

CHAPTER FOUR

Oh, I get it now!

"Oh, my goodness!" she exclaimed. "No wonder I can't make him think my way and understand that it's okay for me to be me, rather than being a carbon copy of him!"

And then: "What a relief! But I still don't like it. I guess if I'm going to be true to who God made me to be, I need to give up my career—and that's a real problem!"

No two people are exactly alike. While two people may be very similar in some areas, they cannot and will not be identical. WHY? The answer has multiple reasons. First, they didn't have the same parents. (And even if they did have the same parents, they were not born under the exact same circumstances.) No two people were born under the same circumstances, of parents with the same thinking styles, nor had the same in-womb experiences. They did not have the same newborn, infant, or early childhood environment or experiences. And they were not given the same gift when they were conceived.

In this chapter we will look at the gift of the four types of brain leads, based on the physiology of the brain. We will examine the four quadrants or chunks of brain tissue, their characteristics and abilities and thinking styles.

For years, we (Ron and Nancy) studied and taught the four temperament types as identified by Hippocrates many years ago. We took the test created and offered by Robert J. Cruise and W. Peter Blitchington and taught extensively by Tim and Beverly LaHaye. We identified our own temperaments. We took training to be able to test others and we taught countless seminars on the subject. But yet, it always seemed that something was missing, we weren't sure just what.

And then we took another inventory. This one identified the quadrant of our brains that are most highly oxygenated. This is important because the quadrant with the higher oxygen worked with greater ease or less resistance, making life easier, less stressful, less complicated, and healthier. We took the training to better understand it, and then went to the originators of the concept and took more training. Still something was missing.

What we finally felt had been missing from each of these inventories was taking into account the in-womb and early childhood experiences of those being tested. We could definitely identify current behaviors; the temperament inventory did that very well. We could look at what the other inventory identified as brain gift, but wondered how much life's earliest experiences impacted the results of those inventories? So we created an inventory using input from the originator of the Brain Lead Inventory, Hermann International, and with their blessing added the component of early life experience. What we have discovered has verified what the ACE Study stated—that *early experience impacts most areas of our lives today.*

Having stated all of this let's look at one couple whose "leads" were so very different.

Rachael was a doctor, a surgeon at that. She was in charge of a very busy practice with three other physicians working for her. Her life was extremely busy and complicated. Richard, her husband, was a pastor of a large inner city church, and had many varied and responsibilities. Dearly loved by his church members and well respected by colleagues and religious leaders, Richard was a hard-working man who tired quite easily.

Their marriage was difficult at best. Conflicting schedules, the high expectations and needs of them both, and two young children complicated their daily life, responsibilities, and schedules.

Then Rachael and Richard attended a seminar for clergy where we were speaking. We had been asked to present information about managing work and relationships, what prevents couples from doing so successfully, and of course, what to do to remedy situations that seemed out of control. We began by teaching about the four quadrants of the brain and how everyone is gifted differently. Prior to our speaking appointment, we had actually tested the people who would be attending our classes and assessed their results to make the classes more helpful for them.

As Richard and Rachael had the results of their inventories in their hands and began to read their assessments and hear us explain this concept, Rachael was devastated. This is when the realization hit her that she was living outside of her original gift, and that by doing so she would eventually pay a huge price physically, emotionally, and relationally. "What can I do?" she asked in a panic-stricken tone.

What had caused her distress? She had just heard us go over the list of things that can befall us when we do not live in the quadrant of our brain most highly oxygenated. She realized that something in her life just had to change, and quickly at that!

Richard was gifted in the **Basal Right** quadrant. People thus gifted are most interested in Harmony. While they are usually very talented and creative, and have a high intellect, their decisions are usually made based on what choice would create the greatest harmony. Music, relationships, color, and harmony of style are uppermost in the thinking of a Basal Right gifted person. This quadrant has the ability to observe facial expression, tone of voice, and body language as major indicators of the character of others. Based on their observations, they are able to determine which path would lead them to safety and harmony. Sensitive to the smallest slights of others toward them or to the feelings of others, these individuals are often the "helpers of the world" who excel in "helping" professions. Careers in the medical field, counseling or psychology, and social work are the most likely, with careers in the arts running a close second.

Rachael was living quite opposite to Richard. She was living in the **Frontal Left Quadrant** of the brain, kitty corner across the brain from where her husband's gift is. Those who excel here make great administrators and analysts. They think logically, seldom incorporating emotion or the feelings of others into their quickly made decisions. The question Rachael wanted answered was if she was living life the way she had been created to live. Many things needed to be taken into account to answer that question.

- Her experience while in the womb
- Her process of being born
- Her relationship with birth parents
- The circumstances of her childhood

Once these questions could be answered, we could determine if she was living life falsely or being true to her gift.

Rachael's mother was not married to birth father. Her birth father left a relationship with her mother early in the pregnancy. Rachael's mother had become an alcoholic, and Rachael recalls that as a young child, barely past toddler stage, having to go to the neighborhood bar to pull her mother off of a bar stool and drag her home. Family meals were poorly scheduled and erratically eaten. Often Rachael assumed the role of caretaker of herself and her mother. She had some aunts who lived fairly close and contributed somewhat to her care, while her mother, because of her alcoholism, was never able to adequately care for her.

Rachael's father was just plain absent. He seldom came around and then only to drop off a small gift for the child and leave again. The bottom line is that at a very young age Rachael became quite responsible, beginning a lifetime of taking charge, being in control, and running her life as well as the lives of others.

Rachael married just the person she needed. We often do, but after the "I do's" are said, we then question if the person we thought was perfect for us does indeed fill that bill. Rachael needed a kind and gentle man; one who would be the father she never had. But the moment he began the fathering behaviors, she was turned off. She needed a strong, decisive man who would provide the security that she missed from her father in childhood. However, when Richard behaved decisively and appeared strong, that ruffled her feathers and she would raise herself up and take charge. After all, she had been used to doing so throughout childhood, and she did it every day at the office and the hospital. Her business, her profession, kept her "on call" most of the time, demanding her attention whenever the phone rang. She longed to be loving and engaging with her children, but the importance of doing so came second to her career demands.

Richard needed a replacement for the loving mother he had lost in his teen years. He still mourned her passing and the affirmation and loving affection she had offered early in his life. He definitely was her "fair-haired boy" and he longed to be treated thus by his wife. As a boy, many of his decisions had been made for him by his parents, albeit his father was not an active participant in his life. Richard's father was a quiet and withdrawn man, who never really modeled to his son how to be a participating, masculine, take-charge father or husband. Rachael could make decisions for sure, and often did, but that seemed to emasculate Richard.

Their time together was limited. Between her schedule and his, and juggling the responsibility of the children and the nanny who cared for them while both parents were at work, Rachael and Richard were both exhausted when they collapsed into bed at night. Where was the time for the two of them? Where was time to communicate? And even if there was time, did they really know how to share thoughts and feelings with each other? Who had taught them how to do it? Who validated her and communicated with Rachael when she was a child so she would feel cherished and special as a young girl? Richard never saw a whole and healthy relationship between his parents, so he didn't know how to relate to his wife. He was trying to get his mother back. It's difficult for two people who come from very different beginnings and whose *Brain Gifts* are so unlike each other's to understand and communicate on a civil plane, especially when they are in what is supposed to be an intimate relationship.

Then Rachael looked at the assessment we had written from the results of her inventory. She was living in a quadrant of her brain that was not her gift, and she was doing so 24/7. When we, as human beings, do that we suffer greatly! It takes a toll on us physically, emotionally, and relationally. In actuality, Rachael was a forward thinker, a creative person, one who can "see" way down the road, predicting outcomes rather successfully, but she was also very concerned with Harmony.

The **Basal Right** or **Harmony** quadrant was being denied in her daily experience. In order for her to live in the **Frontal Left Productive** quadrant, she had to move to that quadrant which also houses the tendency for anger. That caused her to pay a dear price in her marriage and in her physical body as well. Her health had already begun to break down and her marriage was faltering.

Richard was easily offended, easily felt rejected, and found it difficult to decipher why he could be so successful in his career but couldn't seem to make things function well at home. His **Basal Right** gift gave him the ability to be sensitive to others, but his secondary ability to hide in the routine of the **Basal Left** quadrant left Rachael still longing for the father/husband she had been longing for all her life.

Was there a solution? Could this marriage be saved? The solution, which Rachael already had perceived was the best way to resolve what seemed unresolvable. What did she do? She did what was best for her—and thus, her family.

Though she was a very courageous and successful physician, she sold her practice. She determined to stay home with her children, to raise them, to be present for them. She chose to give to them what she had not received from her own mother—physical and emotional presence, love, and acceptance. She studied, and read, and learned about herself from other family members. She applied what she learned about her beginnings to what was happening in her current life. She chose to make the changes necessary to make her life and the lives of her family, less stressful.

Rather than being happy, Richard was aghast by the changes his wife chose to make. For one thing, how would they survive financially?

Their complete story of God's providence in their lives is amazing. From the brink of bankruptcy, God took them to a new home and a job for Rachael that provides more than adequate income to counter the financial losses incurred from changing her situation. And this was accomplished without sacrificing time with her children and her husband. Sure their financial losses were great, but they chose to depend on God who holds the whole wealth of the world in His hands to provide for them. And that He has done!

Richard resigned from the huge inner-city church so that he could live closer to his wife and children and not have to make the two-hour trips back and forth to the church he then pastored. He chose to take a smaller parish and another career responsibility which allows him to make the home, the marriage and the family priority number one.

All of these changes took place because two people decided to look at themselves in the mirror, so to speak. They examined their history, they studied their brain giftedness and they responded according to what would make them work well and be a blessing to each other and to their children.

Lessons Rachael Learned in Childhood:

1. <u>You must take responsibility to care for yourself and others</u>. "When childhood is out of control, adulthood takes control." Very early, Rachael learned that no one was in control in her childhood. Her parent was irresponsible, so Rachael became the parent in the household and learned how to organize and administrate herself and her mother.
2. <u>Count on no one to meet your needs.</u> Take care of yourself. That's great as a single, but in a marriage, the lack of trust that this attitude can promote, can easily play divide and conquer in a relationship.
3. <u>You cannot trust a man.</u> They will leave or refuse any responsibility. If you control them, you'll be safe. Unfortunately, Rachael did not learn in childhood how to communicate with a man. Her father

was absent, so she just took charge in a marriage avoiding the needed communication with her mate.

Lessons Richard Learned in Childhood:

1. <u>Women are supposed to coddle you and take care of your needs</u>. That's what his mother did, while his father was very laid back and non-attentive.
2. <u>Don't share honestly with your partner or children</u>. That's what happened when his mother was diagnosed with cancer and was dying. Richard was not told of her impending death, so it came as a great shock to him. In his relationship with Rachael, rather than sharing feelings and history, he kept it hidden.
3. <u>Men allow women to take charge in a marriage</u>. Richard learned by observing his father and followed suite in his own marriage, all the while resenting his being stripped of the masculine role.

Principle 1: Knowing oneself is absolutely necessary.

A look in the mirror at current behaviors is always valuable. Following the look, ask the question *Why? What set me up to think, feel and behave in this manner?* This is a process, which often painful, is necessary for personal growth and relational healing. Who was the person or persons who taught me this behavior or feeling by direct command or by example? How has what I learned from that person affected me personally? How is what I learned affecting my marriage today? How do I get rid of the drive to keep repeating this behavior or to keep feeling this way, which then forces me to behave in a manner that is not serving me well?

In most cases, <u>we as humans live out of the part of our brain that is designed to survive.</u> Actually, survival is the core issue and mandate of the human brain: to make certain that the brain and the rest of the body will survive at all costs. Unfortunately, <u>when we allow the brain to constantly devote our energy to the techniques that we *think* will allow us to survive, we separate from the heart, which is designed to love.</u>

Our thoughts and feelings as well as our decisions are made from the fear of not being able to survive, instead of out of the love that God places in the heart for us to give to ourselves and to others.

There are only two basic emotions: *fear* and *love*. Fear comes from a brain that is desperate to survive. True love comes as a gift from God to our hearts. The brain, the mind that has been wounded by not having its needs met (remember those 12 Basic Needs?) will instigate *all* of its behaviors out of that emptiness that was not filled: out of fear. The heart, longing to give and receive love, sits idly by just pumping life-giving blood, but not fulfilling its full purpose.

The Bible speaks of this in the New Testament book of James, chapter 1, verse 8. James writes, ". . . a double-minded man, unstable in all he does." The two sides of him, the two body parts warring against each other rather than cooperating, make him (or her) unstable. The internal battle causes the body to break down, the immune system to be compromised, and the mind to be confused.

Ned and Misty are in this situation as we speak. Ned was rejected by his father at a very young age—around two years old. Father divorced Mother and left the family. Then he married a woman who already had two children and became an instant stepfather. After that he was rarely in contact with the son whom he had abandoned.

When Ned was a twelve years old, he traveled to his birth father's home to spend a few weeks during the summer. He was, during that visit, repeatedly molested by his older stepbrothers. When he reported the abuse to his father, his dad denied that the abuse had taken place, and promptly put him on a bus and sent him back home to his mother and his own stepfather. Ned's relationship with his stepfather was very poor and he began to act out against all he had experienced. In his later teens, Ned left home, never to return. But leaving the family house did not enable him to leave behind the painful memories of his childhood experiences. The resulting anger that he experiences causes extreme pain for himself, and definitely for his ill-affected wife and children.

Misty reports having been raised in a "good home" where "none of this abusive stuff" took place, even though the parent's marriage ended when she was just eleven. She recalls sitting at the family dinner table when her father announced that he was leaving. She remembers dashing away from the table, sobbing uncontrollably, and running off to the park to cry. Her older sister came for her, but returning to the house didn't soften the emotional blows. She feared that she'd never see her dad again. Fortunately she reports that after her father left the family he still tried to stay close with his children, taking them out to eat, to the movies, or somewhere special so that they could stay connected.

In their marriage, both Ned and Misty function on fear. When Ned was asked what he most fears in the world, he said, "Loosing Misty and my kids."

Misty answered the same question with her fear—that Ned would leave her and the children by ending his life, which he has repeatedly suggested would be the best thing for him to do.

Despite this situation, Ned and Misty love each other dearly. Neither knows what they would do or how they would survive without each other. They are in a way, double-minded, therefore unstable. They adore each other, but cannot get along. Ned tries to assuage his emotional pain with alcohol, but all that does is loosen his tongue and from his mouth spews derogatory comments and major put-downs. Alcohol has become his "drug of choice," but in choosing it, he is neglecting and ignoring the needs of his wife and children.

In the process of a directed study, and in a small gender-specific group, it is possible to confront personal issues, heal them, and move on to a happy and productive life. The materials in the study will become the template for your needed changes. If you do not have such a group in your area that is doing *The Journey* or *Binding the Wounds,* consider starting a group of friends and acquaintances. Perhaps people you work or worship with would find such a process beneficial to them. Remember, many marriages fail because people do not have knowledge. You would get much needed information in the materials used in the recovery group and would find comrades walking alongside, supporting you as you support them in the process. See www.fixablelife.com to read about and order materials.

Principle 2:

Living life while not accessing the quadrant of your brain that is most gifted, can cause many emotional and health related issues.

The right hemisphere is known as the relational brain. It is:

* **Visual** - Sees everything in picture form
* **Subjective** - Perceives its own reality (may be different from actual)
* **Impulsive** - Instinctive and spontaneous
* **Imaginative** - Has lively imagination
* **Intuitive** - Looks beyond the obvious

The left hemisphere is more logical in its capacity and function.
It is:
* **Functional** - Makes things work
* **Objective** - Deals with facts
* **Analytical** - Skilled in reasoning
* **Deductive** - Draws conclusions by reasoning
* **Realistic** - Factual

Four Brain Quadrants

Each of the hemispheres of the brain has two main areas, a **frontal** and a **basal**. That means that there are four main areas of the brain. These areas have specific abilities and specialties—they are highly specialized chunks: basal (or back) left and basal right, frontal left and frontal right. Each of the four lobes has its own specialized screens or filters that cause it to perceive only what is necessary to do its job.

Each and every day, we use all four quadrants of our brains. Everyone needs and uses the abilities found in each of the quadrants, but usually one quadrant stands out from the four as a personal specialty. Some individuals have two that are highly gifted and a very few are proficient in three of the quadrants. However, in every individual, one quadrant is most highly gifted.

The Frontal Left's specialty is that it perceives function and functional relationships. It excels in what supports what, with what degree of tolerance, and in what blocks what. In other words it *knows* the big picture of what components relate and work together. People gifted in this quadrant want to know each component of a machine, a plan, etc., and want to know how each works with the other to perform a function. They are gifted in logical analysis and can calculate, evaluate, diagnose, and prescribe effectively. In addition, the frontal left chunk excels at directing, prioritizing, and strategizing.

The Basal Left sees bounded shapes or masses that it labels with words it hears and uses. It prefers to grasp and handle in order to produce a product (hands-on work), is specialized in sequencing, and excels at performing routine tasks. It breaks things down bit-by-bit, step-by-step. It can appear to be objectively detached, and can gain control by use of rules, orders, structures, and systems. It processes information and creates things such as: divisions of labor or class, chain of command, color coding, etc.

The Basal Right perceives the presence or absence of harmonic relationships (audio, visual, physical, or kinesthetic—sensation of movement) in its environment, and acts to establish harmony and connection where it is missing. It excels at building good will, trust, and loyalty, and the basis for peace, cooperation, and collaboration. It is very sensitive to the facial expressions, tones of voice, and body language so that the person can create harmonious relationships.

The Frontal Right perceives abstract patterns and relationships, and sees pictures in place of words. It can perceive the abstraction or caricature of a face. It is gifted at seeing trends—this signals change and triggers the imagination to invent a successful response to the change noticed (product, service, strategy). It is superbly suited to help us adapt to change. Children who are gifted in this quadrant are often diagnosed as having ADD or ADHD. They have difficulty sitting still because their body desires and needs to move as rapidly as the ideas and pictures bombarding their minds.

Principle 3:

Living outside of your original gift can and usually will result in the devastating condition known as PASS—Prolonged Adaption Stress Syndrome.

Commonly observed symptoms of PASS include the following, which may be present in varying degrees in individuals who have been Falsifying Type or Adapting (chronically living outside of their giftedness). They are:

1. **Fatigue**— A growing fatigue not alleviated by sleep
   - Increased need for sleep but interference with the quality of sleep
   - Decreased dreaming.
   - Exhaustion
   - Tendency to crave specific foods or high fat/sugar snacks for "quick energy" > weight gain with its stressors.
   - Tendency to self-medicate, attempting to alter brain chemistry (the neurotransmitter ratios). This is often accomplished by alcohol, nicotine, caffeine ingestion.

2. **Hyper-vigilance**—Protective alertness for safety.
   - The brain can be temporarily pushed to introversion. It requires increased energy to maintain this level of alertness (to keep the lens of the brain open wider)

- Increased sensitivity to environmental stimuli (light, sound, odors). This can impact relationships.

- Change in activities. Previously enjoyed activities can be discarded in favor of less gregarious ones. A person may appear to be isolating, but is doing so to decrease stimulation.

3. **Immune System Alteration**—Individual "living a lie" or Falsifying Type.
   - Falsifying type can suppress immune system function (temporarily shrinks the thymus gland)) which can negatively impact one's health. Symptoms can include:
   - Slower rate of healing after cut or abrasion
   - Increased autoimmune disease symptoms
   - Increased susceptibility to illness
   - Increased risk of developing cancer

4. **Memory impairment**—Cortisol, released under stress, can interfere with memory functions.
   - Decreased ability to lay down a memory, to store data in long-term memory or access/recall memory at a later date.
   - Diminished neurotransmitter function—reduces effective neuron communication – the *"phone lines are down"*. The mind becomes *"muddled"* with a reduced ability to concentrate.

5. **Altered brain chemistry**—prolonged adaption can interfere with the hypothalamus and pituitary function, upsetting hormonal balance.
   - Decreased growth hormone
   - Decreased insulin secretion
   - Decreased reproductive functions
   - Increased production of glucocorticoids, prematurely aging the hippocampus (what is used to lay down memories in time and space) .
   - Possible alteration in permeability of the Blood Brain Barrier

6. **Diminished frontal lobe functions**
   - Decrease in artistic/creative endeavors. (ex. writer's block)
   - Reduced ability to brainstorm options

- Reduced ability to choose "best" option in critical situation
- Interference with logical/rational decision making
- Increased injuries due to distraction and/or making mistakes
- Slowed speed and clarity of thinking

7. **Discouragement and/or depression:**
   - Repeated triggering of conserve/withdraw response to stress—especially true for high introverts.

   - Can be seen in extroverts who perceive a mismatch between who they are and society's expectations or repeated failures.

     o 20 million US citizens are depressed. 15 % are suicidal. PASS is a contributing factor in some.

8. **Self-worth problems:**
   - Individual can take on "victim" role or endeavor to be all things to all people

   - Inflated self-esteem—individual takes on an "offender" position or becoming quickly defensive as a result of years of invalidation.

   - The pendulum—individual swings from one extreme to another. Sometimes seen in professional invalidation, but validated personally with a small group of friends. The dichotomy can be confusing, unnerving, and disconcerting as the individual tries unsuccessfully to be seen as successful in both areas.

This material was prepared by Arlene Taylor, Ph.D. and Katherine Benziger, Ph.D. and synthesized by Ron Rockey, Ph.D. and Nancy A. Rockey, Ph.D.

Principle 4: The willingness to seek and obtain help in deciphering your personal and marital dilemmas will change your life for the positive, if you are teachable.

Look at the dramatic results of just one couple whose story you have just read. The ingredients that made their story and their marriage a success was their willingness to take Windex to the mirror and then take a long look. The look would take them back into their history, their beginnings, and into their current culpability for the dysfunction in their lives and marriage, and then into what the future could hold for them if they were willing to put pride in their pockets and make necessary changes.

We include in this book the stories of others so you can compare them to your own. It is also written with the intention that you will also get out the mirror, dust it off, polish it well, and begin to take a long look behind you, right in front of you, and into the future. When you take that look, and you'll need to revisit the mirror time and time again, grasp the courage of Richard and Rachael and take whatever steps are necessary to keep the main thing the main thing. The main thing is your personhood, your marriage, and your family.

IN SUMMARY:

At conception, every person is given a gift of oxygen to the brain's four quadrants. At birth, the quadrant most highly oxygenated is **Basal Right**, so that the child can respond to the parents' bonding by attaching to the parents. That process of attachment is completed by age two.

Later, usually one or occasionally two of the quadrants have higher amounts of oxygen than the other quadrants. These quadrants work with ease, and living in them brings exhilaration, joy, success, and ease to an individual.

When we do not live in the highly gifted quadrant, life become increasingly more difficult, relationships suffer, and our physical body deteriorates too. It is advisable to know yourself well as you enter a relationship. Few people do, but it is never too late to begin the process. Regardless of how your Brain Lead may differ from your mate's, you can still, with understanding and perseverance, work through the differences and use them to your advantage and to the healing and restoration of marital harmony.

If you are interested in taking our MindPrint Inventories, go to www. fixablelife.com and click on MindPrint. There is a cost for the inventories, but they certainly give a complete picture about who you are, so long as you answer the questions honestly.

Questions for You to Answer and Share

1. Having read about the four quadrants of the brain, their gifts and abilities, which quadrant would you say is your gift?

2. What about your thoughts, behaviors, or abilities made you decide which quadrant houses your gift?

3. Which, if any, of the symptoms of Falsification, of PASS do you have? Be honest now!

4. For what reason(s) are you pleased or disappointed in what you think is your gift?

CHAPTER FIVE

Powerful Parents

It is true that the most powerful relationships we have in our lifetimes are the relationships we have with our birth parents. While in the womb and in those first two years of life, the connections we develop with them will create filters that begin the process of molding our character (thoughts and feelings). However, these parental connections have been playing havoc with marriages ever since the beginning of time. In an ideal world, we would have received exactly what we needed, but since we are living in a sin-filled world, and all parents are imperfect, we didn't get everything we needed, and sometimes we got too much of what we didn't need. While our parental connections are supposed to provide us with nurturance, acceptance, and love, there are instances where what we got was a load we could not carry.

In order for a son to develop his identity as a male, he requires the presence of his father, both physical and emotional presence. The father must be present physically for the son to emulate his behaviors and present emotionally during the character forming years, so that a son can identify himself as a male. In order for the son to develop manly qualities he needs a model—a whole, healthy and present father. Because father is his model, father is one of the strongest forces that

> **IDENTITY** is a psychological process in which a subject assimilates an aspect, a property or a characteristic of another, and transforms himself totally or partially on the basis of this model. Webster's New Collegiate Dictionary

dictates to the son his **sexual identity**—"I am a male." When the father is missing emotionally, physically or both, this dictates that the son's sexual identity is fragile. If the father is <u>silent</u> the son has difficulty establishing his own sexual identity.

The absence of the father figure leaves a black hole in the emotional mind of the son, the place where the father should have been. Usually that emptiness is filled with <u>resentment</u> because the father abandoned the son or because he would not connect with him. The son takes the responsibility for the father's behaviors or absence, and feels <u>guilty</u> for his dad's absence. The son's mind becomes occupied with <u>idealizations</u> – how he wishes the relationship was, what having a father would be like, and comparing his life to the lives of his friends who do have present fathers. A sense of <u>mistrust</u> is created in his mind for the male gender. How can a child trust men who will leave or who refuse to connect? The presence of this resentment, guilt, idealizations, and mistrust will skew, distort, or twist the boy's God-given software to honor his father.

What about the mother in the son's life? If the boy's mother is domineering, overly protective, repressive, (meaning that she keeps the boy at a physical or emotional distance), or not present at all, this inevitably indicates that the boy's father is absent, either physically or emotionally. Think about your family or others you know. If mother is any of these things, there is some deficit in the boy's relationship with the father. If Mother is domineering or overly protective, the father is not the leader in the home, allowing the mother to take charge. This automatically heightens the influence of the mother upon the son, causing the mother to carry a burden far too weighty for her to bear.

This combination of circumstances will cause the son to be:

- <u>Immature</u>, especially in later relationships that are supposed to be intimate.

- <u>Overly dependent on his mother</u>, even in adulthood and after he marries.

- <u>Given to anxieties</u> (worries, concerns, angst, nervousness, or unease), depression (sadness, misery, gloominess, or hopelessness), <u>ob</u><u>sessions</u> (fixations, preoccupations, manias), compulsions (coercions, urges, cravings), and <u>phobias</u> (fears, terrors, dreads)

The son ends up with a deep need for love, but without the mechanism to adequately or appropriately express it, so he resorts to:

- Half-hearted attempts at suicide
- Running away from home (of wife and children after marriage)
- Imaginary illnesses; this gets him sympathy
- Wild accusations directed toward others—especially his wife after he marries
- All sorts of manipulations to get his needs met.

Without a father actively involved in his life, the boy grows up without a sense of an internal structure. His ideas are often confused; his thinking perverted. He has trouble setting goals for himself and becoming a success in life. He tends to be indecisive: afraid to make decisions for fear they will be wrong. He has trouble deciding what is good for him, albeit he can usually make decisions for others. He has trouble identifying his own specific needs.

Everything seems to be mixed up for this young man: his love life, his ability to reason, his sexuality, his appetites, and his simple need for affection. Adding to his misery is an inability to concentrate well.

This whole picture often sets up the mother as being the only reference point in his life, and she looms large in his mind and life. He runs the risk of remaining a little boy in relation to his powerful mother. This complicated mess sets the boy to remain fused, or stuck in his childhood unconscious mind. And because he has not been able to mature emotionally, his focus tends to be on his own desires, his own impulses, his own ideas, and he has little or no access to his own individuality. So he remains subject to his unconscious mind and to the whims that live within it.

Having said all of this, let's look at a couple who demonstrates this well.

Leonard and Genevieve, a married couple, carried a load far too weighty to sustain. They had been inadvertently handed this load by their own parents.

Gen was her father's favorite and less regarded by her mother. When Gen married, she "needed" a husband to place her in the princess role her father had assigned her. However, she married at a fairly early age and was abandoned by her husband when he discovered she was pregnant. She gave birth to a son, and they lived with her parents until the boy was just beyond his toddler stage.

Gen's great need for a man in her life caused her to give an abundance of time and attention to her son, Michael. Many would have said that Michael was "spoiled." She would have argued that. But Gen gave him the kind of emotion that should have been saved for a husband. Because a child is not designed to carry the emotion of an adult and the load is too heavy and not understandable, the child inevitably suffers. Especially a male child will feel duty-bound to fix his mother, but of course, a child cannot repair the fractured emotions of an adult. Beneath the age of seven, a child is simply absorbing, not thinking in a logical, problem-solving way.

When Michael was about four years old, Gen met and subsequently married Leonard. Now of course, he came to the marriage with his own issues. Remember, we are attracted to and marry our emotional equal, and that they both did.

Len was the youngest of several children, the son of an alcoholic father and an emotionally absent mother who had had to work outside the home to support her family. With an absent mother and an addicted father—whose attention was given to his drinking rather than to his children—Len had two giant emotional holes to fill. He dated many girls in college and afterward, mostly all of them were the motherly type, before he married Gen.

When Leonard became a husband, he also became a stepfather to Gen's son, Michael, and here entered what appeared to be the cause of their major marital crisis. Gen would not allow Len to discipline her son. Len would seem to tolerate Michael's obnoxious behavior for a while and then, out of an overload of it, would explode. At that point, his treatment of Michael and the words he screamed bordered on the abusive. When in his childhood had he learned fathering skills? How could he have, from an emotionally absent and often physically absent father? The boy *appeared* to be the major source of their disagreements, but in reality they simply focused on the boy and made him their scapegoat. Len and Gen's real issues stemmed from their own poor relationship with their parents.

Finally, both Gen and Len agreed to end their marriage, because no matter how hard they tried, Michael was always the wall between them. *However*, there was another issue which aggravated their relationship much more than Gen's son did. It was that they didn't know or understand the true cause of their difficulties. In the lives of both Len and Gen, there were two people either missing or overly bonded to them in their early years. Carrying this issue complicates the lives of many married couples, but it is hardly even understood or acknowledged. It sets people up to marry the person they hope will fill a giant hole in their lives, but when the attempt for that filling is made, severe complications ensue.

Lessons Len Learned in Childhood:

1. Choose a woman who appears to be motherly. Len's lack of mother-presence and emotional attachment created a great need within him to find a woman who could and would play mother to him and to his children. He did marry a woman who was already a mother, but he did not realize that the powerful emotional connection he observed between mother and son during the dating months would create a bone of contention after their wedding. He did not recognize that the emptiness within him could never be filled from the outside. He expected his wife to fill the emptiness left by his mother—with *something*, but he didn't know what that something was. How could he when he had never experienced love?

2. By his father's example Len learned that men can numb out and do not have to connect strongly to their children. That was certainly the case for him in childhood because his model for manhood, his father, appeared numb, preoccupied with his addiction, and frequently absent. Len's internal structure was faltering and unsteady, so being decisive and a gentle leader in his home was just not possible. Len had a career that allowed him to be absent often from home, and when he was at home he was frequently overly tired.

3. Keep quiet until you cannot handle the internal stress any longer, then blow up! What should have happened in Gen and Len's situation is that an understanding should have been made prior to their union. However, neither were capable of doing that. When we don't have knowledge and we think that love is enough, often we inadvertently miss important things we should know about potential partners before a commitment is made.

> The "Good Book" reminds us that:
> *"[God's] people die for lack of knowledge"* (Hosea 4:6).

Before the day that Len said, "I do" to Gen, he and Gen should have been agreed that since Michael had never experienced a father's love and discipline, it was now time for him to do so. But then, Len had no idea how to be a father. During the engagement period, Gen should have slowly given over the reins to Len. He should have been allowed to adopt the child, give him his last name, and assume the father role. However, if Gen had known enough to do so, she would have inquired in depth about Len's history, what his own father had been like and the type of discipline in his home, and made her decision to marry or not to marry based on their mutual agreement. Len should have done the same, but their desperation clouded their logic. They were drawn to each other by an attraction that neither understood.

Lessons Genevieve Learned in Childhood:

1. <u>That she was her Father's princess and therefore should be the princess to her husband</u>. In a home where the parents' relationship is distant or poor, and a parent chooses a child and bonds to that child in a similar way that a husband and wife would bond, major confusion is created for the child. The child can easily get the message, just by observation and even before language, that the husband/wife relationship is unimportant and that the bond between parent and child is central. This is the message that Genevieve took with her into her second marriage. In fact, she also may have taken that message into her first marriage as well, and that may have been a contributing factor to its demise.

2. <u>Women control men</u>. It's what she saw in her own home in the relationship between her parents and between her mother and her younger brother. She simply copied her mother's behavior both with her husband and with her son.

3. <u>If anything goes wrong in the family, it is always the man's fault.</u> Unfortunately, Gen learned from her mother the lie that she bore no responsibility in any family dysfunction. She learned that she would do no wrong—ever, and that the husband should always be blamed. Unfortunately for her and her children, Gen continued to blame and to demean Len even long years after their divorce. When a parent does this, the children begin to lose respect for the accusing parent, and find it easy to put the demeaned parent on a pedestal.

4. <u>Look and act religious, speak softly and use religious verbiage frequently, and people will believe that you're perfect.</u> That's what her mother did. Unfortunately this is called denial, and denial is a very treacherous place in which to live. One who does fools themselves, not necessarily everyone else.

Principle 1: The ideal for a marriage is created when two emotionally complete and healthy people, whose childhood experiences have been uncomplicated, are attracted to each other.

Sounds good, doesn't it? You wish that were the case for you, right? Well, it can be! In this situation, the male is not unconsciously searching for a partner to be his mother, nor is the female hoping to find a man who will fill the emptiness she feels from an absent or harsh, controlling father. They are able to accept each other on equal terms, with both able to give and receive without great demands for emotional need to be filled.

Looking back on the couples whose relationships we have already examined, you can see that in most marriages where there are relational difficulties there is a need for a mate to fill a parental role. In Ron and Nancy's marriage, Nancy had a harsh and controlling father who had been absent in her first four years of life. In her earliest years, Nancy developed a hole in her heart where her father should have been, and when he did return from battle, that hole was filled with non-acceptance and anger.

Ron had an absent mother who finally did return home when he was almost a year old, but even then he was an ignored and neglected child. Often, beginning when he was four years old, Ron was sent with a quarter to the movies, which back then bought two full length films, newsreels, and cartoons, and a bag of popcorn. That meant to him, "Be gone for the afternoon. We don't want you around here." So in his child heart there were two holes—one for each parent.

Reviewing Keith and Dawn's story, you can see that Dawn had a giant "male-shaped" hole in her heart, caused by the loss of father, grandfather, and brother, while Keith had an overly smothering mother and a giant hole where his dad should have been.

Rachael had a totally absent father and an emotionally absent mother whom Rachael had to "parent." Richard had a smother-mother and an emotionally absent father.

Doris had an abusive father and an emotionally absent mother, while her Dave had an absent father in his early years and a smother-mother.

Remarkable, isn't it, that in each case we have looked at so far, there has been an overly protective or bonded mother or an absent one, and either an absent father or a harsh, abusive one. It's also mind-boggling that the Bible refers to the sins of the fathers being passed down to the third and fourth generation. Now the staggering reports from science indicate that the Bible has been right all along—that we carry the genes from four generations previous to our own. Genes also determine what traits a whole family (such as the grandson, great-grandson, etc.) will have, because genes are passed down on the chromosomes from generation to generation.

It would be good to inquire what your parents, grandparents, and great-grandparents were like. What illnesses did they have? What character traits dominated their behavior? In what ways are you like any of your ancestors? When you understand that traits are passed generation to generation, and that early childhood occurrences and modeling play a rather impacting role in a person's life, you begin to see the importance of knowing what came before you and what you learned from those early experiences.

Principle 2: What a whole and healthy relationship would look like.

5. **First of all, you would have good ingredients.** What? What we mean by this is that both the male and female would come from homes where their father took seriously the roles of <u>Provider</u>, <u>Protector</u> and <u>Priest</u>. This means that he worked to provide food, housing, clothing, medical attention, and perhaps an occasional treat or vacation for his family. He protected them from danger—dangerous people, dangerous objects, and from situations in the world that would cause hurt to be experienced, at least as far as possible. He would also have made sure that if his child was wounded, the perpetrator of that wound would be made accountable. He would be the priest—the one who carries his family's misdeeds to God. As spiritual leader of the home he would teach his children about God and his own characteristics would resemble those of a loving and accepting God.

Also in that childhood home, the mother would have been a <u>concerned</u>, <u>compassionate caregiver</u>. She would be concerned about the physical and emotional needs of her child and would observe the child closely to discern his or her characteristics and specific needs. She would be compassionate: empathetic, kind, gentle, and benevolent, carefully providing a safe and comforting place for the child to run to when he or she felt hurt. Mother would be a gentle giver of care even before the child expressed a need, was sick or injured. She would bathe, clothe, feed nutritious meals, tenderly rock and cuddle when the child needed attention. She would be an active listener, showing interest in what interested the child.

Because of the excellent experiences in childhood and the modeling of healthy parents, the couple would have these qualities:

2. Both male and female would know how to relate, how to meet the other's needs. This knowledge came from growing up in a healthy environment where both Mother and Father were solicitous of each other, respected each other, and showed tender regard and attention toward the other.

3. The husband, who was created to be the *initiator*, would create a bridge to his wife, to meet her emotional needs. WHY? Women are emotional and need a partner who will talk to them about their thoughts and feelings and who will be willing and anxious to hear about her thoughts and feelings. Remember, he would take the place of the priest, of God in the home, and behave in a manner similar to how God treats us.

4. The wife, who feels emotionally filled from her husband, would *respond* to his initiation of intimate conversation by being willing to be open sexually. Many men have difficulty understanding why a woman wants to talk so much and wants to hear her husband speak, sharing his thoughts and feelings with her—sharing who he is. Often this is the case before a woman can feel comfortable in opening herself for sex. The truth is that *his openness begets her openness!* Then and only then is she "in it," and will experience her own sexual delight. Most men are as fulfilled by their wife's sexual pleasure as they are in their own climax. When this is the case in a marriage, both husband and wife are satisfied. The truth is, that the husband can have abundant sex with his wife, but if he has not *initiated* by being open and vulnerable emotionally, speaking and listening to her, those sexual encounters with his wife will not be satisfying or fulfilling to him. Without this ability to give and receive, their sexuality is either just functional, infrequent, or nonexistent.

5. Into this healthy relationship, children are born. In their son's growing up years after his initial focus on mother, the caretaker, his focus shifts to his father, his model. He watches carefully and follows what Daddy does, trying to copy and be like Dad. He will even walk like his father, and if Dad has had a leg injury with a resulting limp, the little boy will even copy the limp.

Out of the corner of his eye however, he also will watch his mother. How does a wife treat a husband? How does a woman treat a man? How does a mother treat a father? This will become his model in later years. He will look for a wife who will be much like his healthy, loving mom.

A daughter will do the same with her mother. She will copy her, walk in her high-heeled shoes, inexpertly apply her mother's lipstick, and play with Mommy's pots and pans. And out of the corner of her eye, she will watch her dad. How does a man treat a woman? How does a husband treat a wife? How does a father treat a mother? And when her time comes to choose a mate, she will invariably choose one who will treat her in the way her father treated her mother.

This was God's original plan. Whole and healthy parents will produce whole and healthy children, who become parents and will produce the next generation of whole and healthy children.

However, when sin entered in the Garden of Eden, this plan began to deteriorate. It actually happened when Adam and Eve had their first two sons. Their relationship with each other was not a great one, because each blamed the other for the loss of the beautiful Garden from which they had been expelled.

Let's look now at the Dysfunctional or Unhealthy Relationship:

A son is born into a family where both parents have been injured in childhood. By "injured" we mean that the father comes from a family where he had an issue with his mother. Now please understand that the issue can, like the pendulum of a clock, swing from one side to the other. Mother could have been absent, harsh and cruel, physically, emotionally, or sexually abusive, or emotionally distant. Or Mother could have been a smother-mother. She, like Gen, and Eve in the Bible, would give wife-like attention to her son, making him into a surrogate husband, a son who carried the emotional load of the mother, listened to her complaints about Dad and her whining about their marital relationship. The boy, designed to be a fixer, tries to repair his mother's poor situation, cheer her up with a dandelion bouquet, or console her by his snuggling closeness but nothing seems to work. He can't fix his hurting mommy, but he remains loyal, listening to her tale of woes and carrying her pain.

Something additionally devastating happens within the male child. Because he has been treated not as a son but as a surrogate husband, sexual feelings begin to arise within him before he can comprehend them. Often at a very early age he becomes a compulsive masturbator in order to compensate for the adult role he is playing in the family. He has very little admiration or respect for his father, the male, and tends to become compulsively drawn to the females. It is possible that he also can create a prejudice against men, and has no idea how to truly be a man without the presence of the ideal father.

The load he is carrying from his mother is far too heavy for the boy to carry, and in that excessive burden he blows an emotional fuse. That explosion causes him to resent female demands, and even become unable to really hear the content of a female's conversation, once he is married.

As he matures into late teens and early twenties, he is strongly attracted to females. He begins to pursue them and seems to know exactly how to walk it and talk it. He is quite a "Casanova" and can charm a female into most anything, as long as it's outside of a committed relationship!

Underneath his assertive and charming behaviors however, he has a fear that usually doesn't expose itself—that he is a failure with women. You see, if his mother was missing as he grew up, or if he was unable to console or fix his mother, he wonders if he can rise above that failure in his marriage. Often however, his mother doesn't want to let him go, and this complicates his feelings of confusion and frustration.

Since we are attracted to our emotional equals, he is attracted to a woman with a "father wound." Simply stated, her father was either absent (Dawn's case) or cruel and harsh (Nancy's situation) or downright abusive (Doris's father), or as in Gen's case, she was the "princess" who got treated by her dad like a surrogate wife. In their dating, this girl will "buy into" the charismatic ways of the boyfriend, either because she is used to those ways from her father or because she is desperate to fill that hole left in her heart by a harsh, cruel, absent, or abusive father. In either case, she is "tied up" in her mind with her father—either out of selfish love or out of anger and resentment. Her boyfriend feels that she doesn't require too much of him, and she doesn't because she is concentrating on either her love for or her distain of her father. She admires her boyfriend's "relationship" with his mother because she'd been taught to find a husband who loves and spends time with and gives attention to his mom.

And so they marry. Shortly after the "I do's" have been said, the relationship they *thought* they had begins to fall apart. He doesn't want to listen to her because she sounds too much like his mother. He becomes angry and even abusive when she reminds him in any way of his mother. In Ron and Nancy's marriage, all Nancy had to do was bake (Ron's mother was a professional baker) and he became angry and verbally abusive. While he loved the results of Nancy's baking, he couldn't seem to stop himself from becoming cruel whenever she did bake. Such men become distant, withdrawn, angry, and verbally or physically abusive, or they stay away from home, working or playing.

Soon the wife's memories from her father seem to be being played by her husband. He is absent. He is harsh or cruel. He is abusive. He will not share his thoughts and feelings intimately with her. Maybe he doesn't meet up to her memories of her princess status. She becomes lonely. If she tries to push her husband for more attention, for him to share thoughts and feelings with her, he becomes angry and resentful and what he shares is a tirade of accusations about her being controlling and pushy. In so doing, he is not only speaking to his wife, but unconsciously to his mother also—his wife is getting the brunt of his resentments toward his mother.

Often couples in marital difficulty will choose to have a child to "fix their marriage," and so they become pregnant. They often produce a son—after all, it's what she needs, and new science now postulates that the egg not only produces a scent to attract either male or female sperm, but will actually open up to receive the exact sperm that the egg chooses.

Because of the mom's great need, she overly bonds to the son she has birthed. When a daughter comes along, the husband will tend to overly bond to her (often because the daughter is the only one available to him since wife is bonded with the son), and the set-up for a repeat of their generation and the previous generation has been established.

When couples choose to marry, they usually do so out of an attraction that is strong but unexplainable by either of them. They just "know" it feels right. But there is so much more to consider in a union of two individuals that is designed to last a lifetime.

Often in the dysfunction we have described here the wife feels unloved and unaccepted by her mother-in-law. In some families it is subtle and in others quite overt. Recall Keith and Dawn's story of her mother-in-law not accepting and actually being cruel to her. What was that about? Mom had picked Keith to be her "chosen" one, the one to whom she gave the heaviest portion of her devotion and her dependence. When Dawn came along, Keith's mother saw her as the adulteress; the one who was taking her fair-haired, chosen son from her. The entire family knew then, and still knows and even jokes about the fact that Keith remains her favorite.

There came a time in their relationship when Keith actually built an addition to their home to be an apartment for his mother. Please understand that money that should have been devoted to his wife and children was being funneled to his mother. Dawn didn't seem to resist that, but what was difficult was the attitude that Keith's mother displayed toward her—it was one of distaste and avoidance. She seldom engaged in any decent conversation with Dawn, and when they did converse, there was always some deliberate "dig" directed Dawn's way.

Often in the situation where the son is emotionally enmeshed with the mother, even after his marriage, mother will want to talk to him on the phone away from the hearing of his wife. She will want him to visit her without the daughter-in-law. She wants detailed information about their marriage and she wants to interfere. She will even do whatever she can to play divide and conquer between them, insisting that her son do all manner of favors for her, without the daughter-in-law present. All of this is designed for Mother to remain the most important person in the son's life, receiving first allegiance and putting his wife in second place. However, Mother may not even recognize or be willing to acknowledge what she is doing. She may honestly believe that she is simply "helping" the son, but her interference into the sacred circle of his marriage is not help; it is hurt, and is absolutely opposite from what God instructs in his word.

IN SUMMARY:

Parents are indeed the most powerful influences on the lives of their children. Regardless of the later experiences and relationships of life, those months in the womb and the first two years of life—when we learn 75 percent of what we need to know for life—affect us more than anything else. We may want to argue that fact, however, in those 33 months, the filters or the glasses through which we will see life are created. For the rest of our years those filters are the interpreters of everything else we see, hear, touch, taste, smell, or experience.

The unhealthy bonds created between mother and son or father and daughter can warp all future relationships, primarily those with the person we marry. They also influence the way we will parent our children.

Questions for You to Answer and Share

1. What teaching from this chapter disturbed you the most?

   Why?

2. Recalling your childhood, who do you feel was your mother's favorite child?

   What makes you think this?

3. Who do you feel was your father's favorite?

   What makes you think this?

4. Being totally honest, which of your feelings and behaviors makes you feel that you <u>have</u> or <u>have not</u> left your parent's household to assign primary loyalty to your mate?

CHAPTER SIX

Grown Up

Think back for a minute. Would you have been able to be a married man or woman, with all of marriage's responsibilities and privileges when you were three years old? No doubt your response to that question is, "Don't be ridiculous!" EXACTLY! However, you will soon see that the question is not as dumb as you may think. Truth is that marriage requires the merging of two adults—physical adults and *emotional* adults. All too often, however, regardless of chronological age, those who marry are emotional children. Emotional children! What in the world are we saying?

In Daniel Goleman's groundbreaking book, *Emotional Intelligence*, he states:

"The personal costs of deficits in emotional intelligence can range from problems in marriage and parenting to poor physical health. [New research shows that chronic anger and anxiety create as great a health risk as chain smoking.] Lack of emotional intelligence can sabotage the intellect and ruin careers. Perhaps the greatest toll is on children, for whom risks include depression, eating disorders, and unwanted pregnancy, aggressiveness and violent crime" (Taken from the book cover).

The amazing thing is that emotional intelligence is not handed to us at birth, but it is nurtured and strengthened or is neglected and weakened by early life experiences. The experiences in the womb, the ability for a child's parents to bond with him/her, the child's observations of his parent's relationship and problem-solving techniques and abilities, and other experiences with significant people such as grandparents and extended family.

Daniel Goldman reports:

"**The high-IQ pure type** (that is, setting aside emotional intelligence) is almost a caricature of the intellectual, adept in the realm of mind but inept in the personal world. The profiles differ slightly for men and women. The high IQ male is typified—no surprise—by a wide range of intellectual interests and abilities. He is ambitious and productive, predictable and dogged, and untroubled about concerns about himself. He also tends to be critical and condescending, fastidious and inhibited, uneasy with sexuality and sensual experience, unexpressive and detached, and emotionally bland and cold."

"By contrast, **men who are high in emotional intelligence** are socially poised, outgoing and cheerful, not prone to fearfulness or worried rumination (pondering or reflection). They have a notable capacity for commitment to people or causes, for taking responsibility, and for having an ethical outlook: they are sympathetic and caring in their relationships. Their emotional life is rich, but appropriate; they are comfortable with themselves, others, and the social universe they live in."

"**Purely high-IQ women** have the expected intellectual confidence, are fluent in expressing their thoughts, value intellectual matters, and have a wide range of intellectual and aesthetic interests. Introspective, prone to anxiety, rumination, and guilt, and hesitate to express their anger openly, though they do so indirectly."

"**Emotionally intelligent women**, by contrast, tend to be assertive and express their feelings directly, and to feel positive about themselves; life holds meaning for them. Like the men, they are outgoing and gregarious, and express their feelings appropriately (rather than, say, in outbursts they later regret); they adapt well to stress. Their social poise lets them easily reach out to new people; they are comfortable enough with themselves to be playful, spontaneous, and open to sensual experience. Unlike the women purely high in IQ, they rarely feel anxious or guilty, or sink into rumination."

"These portraits, of course, are extremes—all of us mix IQ and emotional intelligence in varying degrees. But they offer an instructive look at what each of these dimensions adds separately to a person's qualities. To the degree a person has both cognitive and emotional intelligence, these pictures merge. Still, of the two, emotional intelligence adds far more of the qualities that make us more fully human." (*Emotional Intelligence*, pp. 44, 45).

WOW! Have you found and labeled yourself as one or the other or are you a combination of both? Your findings would make interesting conversation with your spouse, but perhaps you'd better wait a bit until you have practiced dialogue so that you won't be tripped into an argument. This subject has the potential to do just that!

Here's a list for men and one for women. Use it as a personal evaluation of yourself for now. No fair evaluating your spouse just yet. Remember, you've got to look in the mirror first. Even the Bible counsels us to pull the big piece of scrap out of our own eye before messing with the spec in your mate's eye.

Use these lists to check the items that are most like you.

Purely High IQ — FEMALE — High Emotional Intelligence

Purely High IQ	High Emotional Intelligence
____ Intellectual Confidence	____ Assertive & express feelings directly
____ Fluent in expressing thoughts	____ Feel positive about self
____ Value intellectual matters	____ Outgoing & gregarious
____ Wide range of intellectual and/or aesthetic interests	____ Express feelings appropriately
____ Introspective	____ Reach out easily to new people
____ Prone to anxiety, guilt & rumination	____ Playful & spontaneous
____ Hesitant to express anger openly	____ Rarely feel anxious or guilty
	____ Open to sensual experience

MALE

Purely High IQ	High Emotional Intelligence
____ Ambitious and Productive	____ Socially poised
____ Predictable and dogged	____ Outgoing/cheerful
____ Untroubled with concerns about self	____ Not prone to fear/rumination
____ Critical & Condescending	____ Committed to people & causes
____ Fastidious & Inhibited	____ Take responsibility well
____ Uneasy with sex and sensuality	____ Sympathetic & caring in relationships
____ Unexpressive & Detached	____ Rich emotional life
	____ Comfortable with self & others

Have you checked those items that apply to you? If you are fearful, make your check marks in pencil so that they can be erased if you fear that someone else will see them and use them against you.

One of the major contributors to becoming emotionally intelligent, which you can do if you are willing to work, is to **know yourself.** When you can become self-aware, you will have an ongoing attention to your internal states. In such self-reflection, you chose to investigate your experiences and the emotions connected to them. According to Goldman, *"self-awareness is not an attention that gets carried away by emotions, overreacting and amplifying what is perceived. Rather it is a neutral mode that maintains self-reflectiveness even amidst turbulent emotions. It a slight stepping back from the experience, a parallel stream of consciousness that is "meta": hovering above or beside the main flow, aware of what is happening rather than being immersed and lost in it"* (*Ibid.* p. 47).

This awareness becomes an emotional competence on which other abilities such as emotional self-control, is built. According to John Meyer from the University of New Hampshire, and Peter Salovey of Yale University, *"Self-awareness can be a non-reactive, non-judgmental attention to inner states"* (*Ibid.*)

Simply said, self-awareness is looking at your own inner state of being without making emotional value judgments on yourself; not condemning or demeaning or extolling yourself.

Many people live what we term a "reactionary life." They are constantly reacting to some stimulus around them. We all tend to do this to a degree, but in many cases the stimulus to which we are reacting is unknown to us. Remember Pavlov's dog that saw a piece of meat, heard a dinner bell chime, and reacted by salivating? Soon after numerous sights of the meat and sounds of the bell, the German shepherd salivated when he only heard the sound of the bell without the presence of meat. This is known as a conditioned response.

We are similar to that dog. We react without really knowing why. The truth is that the root of your reaction may lay buried deep in your memory and may refer back to an incident that occurred in infancy or in your toddler years, or to an accumulation of experiences

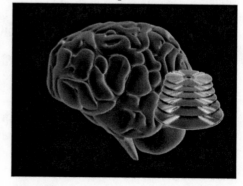

throughout childhood. When a stimulus comes from the outside world, or even from some internal memory that has been inadvertently opened, we automatically go into our huge stack of memories, pull out those that are related to the stimulus and react not only from the present moment, but from every other memory and primarily the old memory that is most highly full of emotion. Believe it or not, our negative memories and the emotions associated with them have the most profound reactions.

Here's what to do when the emotion washes over you:

- Identify the emotion

- Ask yourself, "When in childhood did I feel just the way I feel now?" "Yea, right," you say, "I am going to do just that when I am hot under the collar. Are you crazy?" But really—you CAN do it!

- Once you have that memory, tell yourself, "*That was then and this is now. I don't have to react out of then and now. I can just logically deal with what's happening now.*" Of course, if you have removed the negative emotion from that difficult experience, deciding to separate the old away from the new and responding only to the new in an appropriate manner, it is a whole lot easier.

Here's an illustration from the history of our marriage . . .

It was the Sunday after Thanksgiving, and I was baking. Ron came upstairs to the kitchen from his lower level study and asked what I was baking. "*I thought I should start those gingerbread boys that we give to the children of the church at Christmas. We have so many children, and since they all get three cookies, I'll have to bake in several sessions, freeze them, and decorate them later.*"

"*Are you baking any for us?*" he asked.

Now I was in trouble and I knew it. You see, his mother had been a professional baker, and on the weekends during his childhood, she would make a huge batch of fancy rolls and coffee cakes, and on Saturday nights and Sunday afternoons, friends and neighbors would come for coffee and goodies. Ron was always grabbed by his hair and dragged to his room where he was locked in for the duration of the visits. He and the other kids got only the leftovers on Monday. The fresh goodies had been picked over and he was not included in the enjoyment of freshly baked goods.

It felt to me that no matter how I answered his question, I would be wrong. I was already weary and to bake a batch just for us was "over the top" in my book. I answered sheepishly, *"Gingerbread boys are always a trial in that legs and arms and heads break off. But we can have all of the broken ones.""*

He was not a happy camper with that answer and he blew up. *"That's it!"* he shouted. *"Always the leftovers; never the good things for me. Just like in childhood!"*

For the first time in history I answered him with a challenge. *"How many more Christmas and other holidays are you going to make me miserable because of what your mother did to you?"* I asked him.

He did not respond, but turned on his heels, marched back down the stairs, and slammed the study door.

We are glad that the story doesn't end there. You see, we had already begun recovery and our marriage had greatly improved, so two hours later, as I stood at the sink washing the baking pans, he came and put his arms around me. *"I'm sorry, Honey,"* he said. *"That was a big overreaction. Guess I did pull up old childhood stuff and reacted out of that. This kind of behavior ends today!"*

This is what we told Ned today: *"Tell yourself, 'this is my mate, not my mother.'"* Keep saying to yourself over and over if you have to. Remind yourself of all the ways that Misty shows her love to you. When you recognize that "that was then and this is now," and that Misty is not the one who originally caused your pain, you can diffuse the bomb in your head that is itching to explode. Then tell her what just happened. Tell her that you were able to stop yourself from exploding by reminding yourself that she is your wife who loves you."

"Voicing your experience and tagging it with the victory you have just won, makes a fabulous victory memory in your brain. When the temptation arises again, you now have a memory of victory in the list of failures. The more victories you experience, the easier it is to choose getting beyond the old behaviors, and you'll discover a more pleasant and successful way of living."

IN SUMMARY . . .

Growing up can be hard to do when the wounds received in childhood are unattended and unhealed. The wounds cause us to get stuck at the age the wounding occurred, and we have a hard time moving on to accomplish those tasks that will create in us a sense of hope and drive, instead of carrying around doubt of self and others. We have a hard time developing willpower and the ability to make decisions, so we end up feeling shameful. Feeling that there is a purpose for our existence and that we can establish an altruistic purpose for our lives is a difficult task, leaving us feeling guilty. This is called <u>arrested emotional development</u>.

However, growing up and maturing to the place where marriage can be give and take and not just about satisfying personal needs and wants, can be accomplished. You have just read about a couple who was able to do that and about another couple in the learning process. We have every confidence that you, like many other couples, can become mature if you put your heart and your energy into it. Keep on learning, because KNOWLEDGE IS POWER!

Questions for You to Answer and Share

1. As you look at the three listed stages of maturity and the attributes to be gained, trust, autonomy and initiative, how well do you feel you've accomplished trust?

2. Write a list of five people that you trust implicitly:
    1.
    2.
    3.
    4.
    5.

3. What was the most difficult decision you have ever had to make?

4. What process did you use to be able to make it?

5. When a negative emotion arises, how do you react to it? What do you do?

CHAPTER SEVEN

Self on the Throne

Putting your pride, your will, and what you want in your pocket is not an easy move, but for couples to get along with each other, for marriage to be a partnership, compromise is imperative. To comply with God's instruction, each partner must be willing to occasionally concede their own personal idea or direction to the partner or be willing to compromise, giving up some of what she or he wants. As you are no doubt aware, many people are unwilling to do that. Today's theme seems to be like Frank Sinatra's phrase in the song he made famous , singing, "I did it my way!" You've heard the expression, "My way or the highway," and no doubt have seen or heard a child screaming in the department or grocery store because Mom or Dad is refusing to let them have their own way or buy them the trinket that they want. You may not have seen an adult behaving publicly in that obnoxious a manner, but rest assured many do behind the four walls of their house. Pouting, sulking, hollering, seeking revenge, withdrawing, or distancing, and even physical violence are ways that adults often behave like little children. "I want what I want when I want it, or else!"

Earlier in our ministry, a couple wanting marriage counseling came to us and begged for an appointment. So they came to the office, obviously quite up tight and anxious to get to the heart of their issues. We listened carefully for more than an hour, and felt that their issues were not major, but they both were stubbornly attached to making the other one wrong, the fault, the problem.

After the first hour had passed, we clearly explained our position to them. We told them that we would be happy to teach them the needed techniques to communicate so their feelings could be heard by the other, rather than each making the other person wrong. We assigned each of them the responsibility to have the specific issue that most concerned them about their marriage ready for the next appointment.

When they arrived the next week, we taught them the art of dialogue, of sharing thoughts and feelings rather than accusing or blaming. Then it was time for them to practice. They each had chosen their topic and the wife was instructed to begin with "I am feeling . . . " or "When this happens, I feel . . ." and she was to follow with a feeling word, such as sad, frustrated, disappointed, angry, etc. However, neither of them could do it. They managed to get their first sentence out properly, but their dialogue quickly eroded. Multiple times they started over, but neither could get beyond their drive to make the other wrong, and to use accusatory language.

Aaron and Kattie met when Kattie was still married to her abusive husband, and wishing she wasn't. She was attracted by his boyish good looks and his friendly smile. She was already a mother of two and almost ten years his senior, but to Aaron, that was attractive, because he was unconsciously looking for and needing a mother figure. Even though Kattie was older, she was a beautiful woman who presented a sensual style, and Aaron was hooked! Her divorce was in process, so dating each other didn't seem to present a problem to them.

Both had been raised in religious homes and taught high morals, but both had endured major traumas, causing them to distance from their church and the moral standards taught there. Both had experienced difficulties in their own homes as well as sexual abuse, physical abuse, and definitely emotional abuse. Often when childhood is out of the control of the child, in adulthood the controlled become very controlling. This was the case for Kattie. There was very little that she couldn't do—cooking, cleaning, baking, parenting and working outside the home—all while appearing so attractive to Aaron.

The need to be in control and have need for very little from others is typical behavior for many who have experienced abuse. Another reaction to childhood abuse is anger; after all, abuse is unjust and especially to a child who is in the learning phases of life. Aaron was angry; actually, rage came easy to him! His behaviors vacillated from temper tantrums to numbing himself with drugs or alcohol, greatly complicating their relationship and their parenting.

Kattie wanted to be in charge, but at some level felt that Aaron should be the one in charge. Aaron wanted to be in charge, but had no idea how to do so, especially with such a capable wife. The more she was angry and controlling, the more he drank and drugged. The more he drank and used street drugs, the angrier and more controlling she became. They were on a vicious merry-go-round, with neither one knowing how to slow down or stop the ride. She wanted what she wanted—for him to stop drinking and settle into proper husband and father roles. He had no idea how to do so because his father had not modeled it when he was a child. He wanted what he wanted—a wife who would stop controlling while at the same time would care for all the household responsibilities. He wanted to drink and be stoned so that he didn't have to deal with her control and his out-of-control painful thoughts and feelings. Both were centered on what they were doing in an attempt to survive and to have their needs met.

Lessons Kattie Learned in Childhood:

1. **Work hard and be strong and tough.** While a little girl, Kattie's father demanded perfection. She learned early how to iron, and do so precisely using the method that he demanded. Even though his shirts were perfectly ironed, if she didn't iron using the progression he had taught her, he would become violently angry. Perfection became important.

2. **When childhood is out of a child's control, in adulthood you take control.** Kattie learned to take charge, to do most things very well, to cook, to clean, to care for children, to work at a job (whatever that job was). She knew how to run a household well, and run her husband too. He couldn't handle that! So he reverted back to childhood behaviors, to run away and hide, and that he did in alcohol or drugs.

   It was when Kattie had healed sufficiently and, calling upon her religious training, was willing to let God control her and her husband that their relationship dramatically improved.

3. **Men are dangerous! They control, demean and break your heart, so always be "top dog" over them!** Kattie formed an internal law in childhood that disallowed her to take instruction or bossing from any man, having grown up with a dad who controlled harshly. Her experience of sexual abuse as a child, also contributed to the notion or personal life rule that she had to be a few steps ahead of every male human being. To her, that was the only way to stay safe and in charge. Unfortunately she also learned in childhood that her worth and value were not only tied to her perfectionism, but also to her sexual performance. Through sexuality, she could control most men.

Lessons Aaron Learned in Childhood:

1. **Men do not get involved emotionally in family life.** Aaron was raised in a family where Dad worked his 9 to 5, or more like 9 to 9, and just wasn't involved in the affairs of the home. Sometimes he was gone driving truck for most of the weekdays. He was not a decision-maker, and allowed Aaron's mom to make decisions and run the household. He was equally uninvolved in the lives of his children, so Aaron grew up in a home with a dominant, albeit emotionally distant mother and a passive/absent father. He was naturally drawn to a "take charge" woman, yet when Kattie would "take charge," he resented the control. He felt emasculated. He had not been taught how to be a father, since his own was uninvolved, so when he married Kattie and her two children, he had no clue how to take up the father role. The responsibility felt overwhelming.

2. **Women are oppressive!** When a boy is raised in a family with a dominant mother and an absent or emotionally distant father, mother becomes his only reference point, and she looms large in his mind and often in his life. At some level, always being his mother's confidant and "honey-do" around the house sets him up for dysfunction when he marries. When he marries and his wife employs the same wife-appropriate behaviors, he resents her "control" and "orders." He just wants to be a boy. He wants to play or to party since he didn't ever have that privilege in childhood. Or he will work hard, but resents any behavior on the part of his wife that is reminiscent of his mother's. He doesn't want to carry any burdens his wife has, because he's sick of carrying a woman's "stuff."

   In their marriage, Aaron could be a hard worker and quite proficient in whatever he attempted. His skills had landed him some well-paying jobs, and financially they seemed okay.

3. **Happiness is an elusive dream.** In Aaron's childhood situation, the family moved around quite a bit, following his Dad's employment opportunities. He never saw either parent being happy, being content with who they were, what they had, where they were going, where they lived, or what they were doing. Perhaps they just had no idea who they were or what their goals, dreams, or preferences were, but they just never seemed really satisfied with their lives.

And so it was with Aaron. He had a hard time deciding on a life goal, a plan, a college degree, or something to do with his life that would create some sense of happiness or contentment. His lack of self-worth paralyzed him to a degree; made moving forward in the confidence that he could accomplish anything, a perplexing fear.

Put these two together and you have a disaster. Kattie needed to be in power and control, and that reminded Aaron too much of his mother, so he resisted her.

It was at their lowest point, that we became acquainted with Kattie and Aaron, and began to work with them in an intensive workshop that we occasionally facilitate, entitled EIDO (the biblical Greek word for an intimate knowing of oneself). They were trapped in a relationship that wasn't functioning well, all the while sustaining a love-of-sorts for each other and sheer determination to somehow make their marriage work. The seven 12-hour days, while exhausting, were the knock that finally urged them to open the door to a new life. It was in that experience, the aftermath of continued ah-ha's and their choice to become involved in ongoing recovery, that they began a major turn-around.

Today Kattie and Aaron not only facilitate gender-specific classes of *The Journey,* our recovery program, but they also have made a 4,600 mile journey to move to where they can be mentored, so that when we can no longer teach, they can. Life still presents its challenges as it will for every human being, but with their hands firmly grasping God's hand, they are a new and improved version of what they once were. As Kattie would say, *"You gotta' stay in the conversation of recovery if you want the mind and heart to stay ever-improving."*

Principle 1: Self on the Throne

When babies are born, they come with a built in mechanism for making their needs known. God knew what He was doing for sure when He gave children the ability to know when they are hungry, tired, in need of a diaper change, and needful of affection and holding. Had children not been given this mechanism,

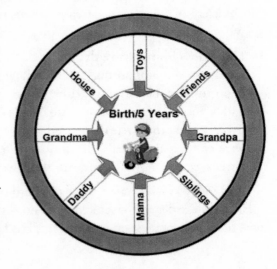

they would lay in their crib, making no sounds, hungry, frustrated, and getting a nasty case of diaper rash!

The human brain is designed to see to it that the brain, the mind, and the body will survive at all cost. This is an inborn mechanism that assists with physical as well as mental/emotional survival. In childhood, the child is in the center of the wheel of life, and everyone else and every other thing revolves around the child, serving him whatever he needs. His mother provides his caregiving, his father provides his security, and siblings (if they are older) model what steps he should take next. Mom and Dad, Grandma, Grandpa, the church, friends, God, and society as a whole are his servants. He becomes accustomed to this, and deviating from it takes appropriate teaching and time to practice caring for others and their needs, during the appropriate stages of development.

Knowing how to get one's needs met comes in very handy in infancy and childhood, but there comes a time when the world needs to stop revolving around the child.
It is time for the child to remove himself from the center of the wheel of life and become one of the supportive spokes. That time is around nine years of age. In order to make this move, the child's parents will have had to teach the child from early on just how to care for others, how to defer to others, and so on. Instead of expecting God to serve

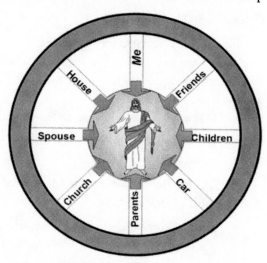

him 24/7, the child puts God in the center of his life and he and all the others on the spokes of his wheel of life, serve God. God no longer has the distinction of being the Sugar Daddy in the sky, but instead there is cooperation between God and the child. He counts on God to "supply all his needs according to His riches in glory," as He has promised to do. He forms a love relationship with God and they become a team that draws others to God. That's how it's supposed to work. Of course there is a requirement here—that the child has learned of God, begun to form a relationship with Him, and has been taught the importance of serving or ministering to others—their feelings, their needs. This is learned by observing his parents interact with each other as well as with himself, and by what he is taught about God.

Principle 2: Getting Off the Throne

It is definitely not as easy to get off the throne as it is to get on it and stay there. Exactly how much energy does it require to work your way off that hot seat? Answer: Quite a lot! Undoing a lifelong habit such as smoking or sucking your thumb is not easy, but remember, you have all the power of God available to you to make such changes. You will need to repeatedly "do it right" to establish your new habit—your new attitude and behavior—but so what! Life will work a whole lot better for you when you do the right thing. This process is working in cooperation with God for your personal recovery.

Principle 3: The How-to Do It

First it is necessary to recognize that's where you are. You look around you and if you can make a list of people who are "dancing to your tune," you are on the throne. What do we mean by "dancing to your tune?" Well answer these questions . . .

- Is there someone who prepares all your meals for you?
- Do you have someone who makes the bed you sleep in every morning?
- Do you have someone who does your laundry—washing, drying, folding, and ironing?
- Is there someone in your life on whom you have put stipulations for your acceptance? Conditions such as:

  * *If you make the food I like, I will love/accept you.*
  * *If you work outside the home bringing in money so I can have my 'trinkets' and the things I want.*
  * *Do all that I want you to do for me; I will love and accept you.*
  * *If you have sex whenever I want to, then I will love and accept you.*
  * *If you don't pressure me to do work around the house, I'll be pleasant to you.*

Of course, as you read the list, you may be guilty of some of these things, but might not admit it. It's hard to recognize our own faults, isn't it? Maybe those questions are subject for future dialogue between you and your significant other.

Step 1: Look in the mirror and recognize the truth about where you are and what behaviors you have. Write a list of the people you have counted on to meet all your needs and conform to your stipulations.

Step 2: Now on a separate piece of paper or in a notebook, see if you can write about who met your needs in your younger years, who met your needs in your teen years, and what specific needs they met.

Step 3: Write a letter to each of these people. WHAT? Hold on a minute. These letters are NOT for sending! They are to be written to empty the need to make others responsible for what you want and what you think you need. They are for telling the one you have made responsible, that you are taking personal responsibility for your future. Now take that letter, or those letters, to a friend, counselor, pastor, or mentor (same sex as you) and tell them you need them to just listen as you read aloud what you have written. An outline of such a letter follows:

Dear _____,

I am writing this letter to apologize to you for making you responsible for me, my happiness, and my future.

I have done this by . . . (Here you list all the ways you have made this person responsible for, things you are really responsible for)

I am asking you to forgive me, because I realize that I have wounded you by . . .

In the future I am determined, with God's powerful assistance, to . . .

Most sincerely,

_____   _____

You may send this letter or you may read it aloud to the person to whom it is addressed.

Step 4: A dialogue with your mate. This is where you share your feelings about what you have recognized in yourself—your responsibilities you handed to others and the stipulations you have placed on your relationships. Ask him/her how those added responsibilities and stipulations have affected her/him. When she/he tells you their truth, do *not* be defensive. Just swallow or as a friend of ours would say, "*Shut up and duck.*"

Then ask your partner what responsibilities you could assume that would benefit him/her. Make an agreement as to what he/she should say or do if you neglect the responsibility you have assumed. Remember, this is not an argument. It is simply contracting with someone close to you – nothing more, nothing less.

Step 5: Write about what it feels like to be taking more responsibility. Share with your partner the feelings that come up inside you when you do what you have contracted to do.

Step 6: Regularly thank God for the changes being made in your life—in your feelings and your behavior. Should you goof, and you can be sure that you will, don't beat yourself up. Just apologize to whomever you have hurt, and thank God that you have recognized your goof and that He is giving you the power to overcome the "old paths"—the old attitudes and behaviors.

Rest assured, you can and will make progress if you keep on, keeping on. The tendency is to easily get discouraged, to want to give up and revert to an "easier" lifestyle, but just keep remembering that you can count on God to keep you progressing in the right direction. Your "goof" was only a needed u-turn. That's it, nothing more!

Questions for You to Answer and Share

1. When you were a child, who catered to you, giving you not only what you needed, but whatever you wanted too?

2. Recall an incident where you had a tantrum or you manipulated until you got your way. Write about it here.

3. If you had to present evidence before a judge and court that you are an emotionally mature adult, what would you offer?

4. Who is the person that offers you what you need without you having to demand forcefully or manipulate?

CHAPTER EIGHT

God's Formula

In the very beginning of time, God instructed Adam and Eve and all couples ever afterward, how to have success in marriage. His formula for success is what we like to call the *Sacred Circle*, and is recorded in Genesis 2: 24 and 25. This sacred circle begins to be created when a man and woman decide to spend the rest of their lives together. It is God's formula designed to insure that husband and wife will create a tight, well-bonded unit where God's character of love and acceptance is constantly revealed and where oneness is assured.

"Therefore a man shall leave his father and his mother, and shall cleave until his wife: and they shall be one flesh. And they were both naked, the man and his wife, and were not ashamed" (Gen. 2:24, 25), KJV.

There are 4 ingredients to this formula. They are: LEAVE, CLEAVE, UNITE, and BE INTIMATE.

LEAVE: In its original language, Hebrew, it means an actual physical leaving. It's as if God was saying to Adam and to every husband-to-be after him, that he must get out of his father's abode, and create a dwelling of his own to which he will bring his new wife. He must make that separation so that his parents will not be interfering in his relationship with his new bride. Believe it or not, many husband's mothers would do just that if the son and his wife were under her nose, so to speak. Mothers, who have an emotionally distant or silent relationship with their husbands, fear the loss of the only man who will listen to her—her son.

As a matter of fact, today in parts of Italy, the marriage rate is dwindling and so is the birth rate. Why? It's diminishing because the son's mothers want the new daughter-in-law to come to live in the parents' home, and be directed how to perform wifely duties by the mother-in-law! How many brides today would be thrilled about that idea, or even willing to allow it, even if only for a short time? The son and perspective daughter-in-law are told that they will *"inherit the family farm and/or fortune if you comply,"* but still few will do so.

CLEAVE: It's quite an amazing word, actually. Both in the original Hebrew language and in Webster's Dictionary, it has two meanings and they are exactly opposite of each other. The first definition is to separate at a natural point of separation the way a meat cleaver separates muscle from bone. The opposite meaning is to glue.

It is as if God was saying, *"Look men, I told you to get out of Dodge, to leave your parents' home, and to move to a place of your own. Now I am telling you again, because it is that important. Not only must you leave physically, but you must leave emotionally. You MUST emancipate yourself from the "hold" that your parents have on you so that your first allegiance can go to your wife."*

Does that mean that you now have no love for or loyalty to your parents? Absolutely not! It simply means that you give top priority to your wife. You take care of her first with your provision, your protection, and your priesthood. There is a scientific truth that *no two things can occupy the same space at the same time.* This is true also in marriage! Never can two different partners occupy the mind and the heart at the same time. Mother and son do not go together like a horse and carriage after marriage. That love belongs now to a wife, and so the song can be sung, *"Love and marriage . . . , go together like a horse and carriage."* That's the love of a wife or a husband, not the love between parent and child. This doesn't mean one must abandon a parent, it simply means that the parent becomes secondary to the mate. That love includes protecting your wife and children from your mother if she would harm or control them in any way.

Notice an important point here. *It is the man who is instructed to do the leaving,* not the woman. Why is that? Shouldn't she give her first allegiance to her husband? Absolutely so, but the reason that the man has the command is that he is designed by God to be the *initiator.* Women are designed to be responders. If you leave your parent, men, and give first allegiance to your wife, she will *respond* by doing the same.

"Wait a minute!" you might say. *"My wife wants to live nearer to her parents than I get to live near mine."* That might be, but . . . have you really given to her the devotion of providing, protecting, and being the priest of the home? If you have, then she will leave her family. *If she is demeaned and insulted, unfavorably compared to your mother or physically wounded by you, her natural instinct will be to run back to Mom and Dad for the protection she felt as a child.*

Remember hearing advertisements for a super glue? In the instructions for gluing two items together, it will always say that the two items must be clean—free of debris, dirt, grease, etc, right? Well, to be honest, it's the same thing when a husband and wife marry. They must come to the relationship clean, unencumbered by old relationships (that means old mates, parents, or boyfriends/girlfriends too).

First of all, we know that you came with physical and character traits from four generations before you, and that was enough of a load to carry. But adding to it what you learned from modeling created quite an overload, didn't it?

A couple with whom we have been working recently, Abby and Enoch, came from very difficult backgrounds. Both of them had issues with both their parents and both came to their marriage as their second. Abby was the eldest girl in her family. Her father abandoned the family when she was a toddler, so that she has in her mind's eye only an occasional glimpse of his face. Her mother became an alcoholic, and in order to support her addiction, she would bring home men from the bars, fall asleep in her drunken state, and these men would use Abby for their sex toy. She had been repeatedly raped by these strangers, and her attempts at reporting this abuse to her mother fell on deaf and denying ears.

Enoch was the son of a man who occasionally was a preacher. He would preach for several years, and then give up the pulpit for the casino and the bottle. He was angry, and in his anger would demean his son, and be physically very cruel to him, while preaching to the boy. At one time, the cruelty was so intense and the boy's rage so peaked, that he took a knife into his father's bedroom and was going to kill him. His father awakened and pulled a pistol from under his pillow and put it at his son's head. Enoch was so distraught that he told his father, *"Go ahead and kill me. Pull the trigger, 'cuz if you don't, I'll kill you for sure when I'm older!"*

Enoch's mother lived with this craziness and was more than a bit dysfunctional herself. She had to go to work to help feed the family, but would beat Enoch and then chain him to his bed before she went off to work. There he would stay for the day until either his mother or father came home.

Would you think that bringing all these memories of pain and childhood agony to a marriage would promote marital happiness? Of course you wouldn't! Enoch came with a gender prejudice against women *and* men. How could he have learned trust in those first eighteen months of development? Abby also brought a prejudice against both genders. Her mother, her model had betrayed her and denied the abuse, and her father had abandoned her. Neither gender was to be trusted by either of them.

But you see, the Lord made it clear in his formula for marital success that we are to leave, to separate at a natural point of separation, so that we can glue in a permanent bond to each other. That means dealing with the painful memories in a recovery process so that you can leave their resulting behaviors behind too.

In Biblical days, when God called Abram to leave the city of Ur of the Chaldeans, He instructed him to "*leave your country, your people and your father's household and go to the land I will show you*" (Genesis 12:1). Abram and his whole family were pagans. His father, Terah, was a pagan priest. Interesting that the God of the Universe was calling a pagan man, and more than that, instructing him to leave his family and in particular, his father's household. God had a plan, and the plan was for Abram to leave behind the experiences of his earlier years, and the relationships that would thwart God's plan for Abram's life. Unfortunately however, Abram did not fully follow God's instruction, and because he didn't, he was waylaid for 205 years in Haran until his father died. God had planned to send him to the land of Canaan, but Abram's choice to allow Lot and his father to accompany him, delayed God's plan for making Abram's name great and making him a blessing. That is why God is saying, "*You must leave!*" If you choose to NOT follow God's instruction, you may end up in a worse condition than a detour. It could be more like a disaster!

How many times we, too, do not do as God instructs. We do not deal with and then forsake the memories recorded in our father's household, and we allow them to fester in us and to dictate to us how we should feel, think, and behave. Often our unwillingness to let go of what was, sets us up for experiencing difficulties in what is. Truth is, if you follow God's instruction, men, you will be a blessing to your wife, your children, and society as a whole. You will not have a divided, confused mind.

Do you, like Abby and Enoch, have difficulty believing in a loving, merciful God? Their only "gods" when their thoughts and feelings were being formed, were cruel or disserting. How about your parents who stood in the place of God for you in childhood?

How could Enoch and Abby, or any others who endured childhood wounding, know what to do to make marriage work? Who taught them God's design, and even if they were taught, how do they get beyond the pictures and feelings in their mind and body? How can they raise their own children with God's principles of love, when they don't really know what love is? How can they know what love is if they didn't experience it in the period of time when they were learning 75 percent of what they needed to know for living life?

Simply stated for now, it would take a concerted effort on both their parts to get beyond the old pain and find the freedom of acceptance from God, from each other, from their children, and from others. Fortunately, Abby and Enoch have begun that work.

Let's return now to that formula set down by God as instruction in the Garden of Eden.

The first ingredient is **LEAVE,** a physical departure.

The second ingredient is to **CLEAVE.** The first part of the cleaving is to separate at a natural point of separation the way muscle is separated from bone. The second part is to glue, to come to the relationship free of old junk, old relationships. It's like God was saying, "Listen boys, I have told you to move out of your mom and dad's home to form a new one of your own. And now I am telling you that you must separate in such a way that first allegiance goes to your wife. That's with whom it belongs!"

Since first allegiance goes to the partner, there must be no secrets between you, except perhaps for the gift you're planning for a birthday or Christmas, or a surprise date or trip. There should be no relationships made that the partner is unaware of or not involved in, unless they are clients in your business or patients for whom a nurse or physician-partner is caring. There should be no hidden money stashed away somewhere for safekeeping, away from the knowledge of the partner. Hidden agendas, hidden relationships, hidden bank accounts are grit, dirt, or grease that will prevent a tight and lasting bond. You see, God's plan was that the two should become one; one in body, mind, heart, and purpose. Healthy living is about sharing not about holding back or hiding.

UNITE (and the two shall become one). This is where you say, "Well we are managing to get this piece right!" But are you? Do you truly know what this business of uniting really means? If you are thinking that this is about sexual union, you are correct, but . . . only partially correct. Two people or two animals can have sexual relations, but do they really "become one?" Isn't there more to you and your partner than your genital organs? Don't you each have a mind (brain) and a heart? So when two become one, is it accomplished in the back seat of a car or even in a luxurious hotel room? Or perhaps it—like recovery—is a process that doesn't occur in a minute, or an hour, or even in a year, because it is more about the process of the union of two hearts. This is true nakedness.

Okay, here's the real scoop. When two people unite sexually, the female's vagina must accept the semen of the man, which is alkaline, while her lining is acidic in nature. Occasionally a woman will have an allergic reaction to semen. However, repeated sexual experiences with the same partner will usually correct the problem as she becomes desensitized. The greater problem occurs when a woman is sexual with multiple partners. There is ever-so-much more to two people becoming one!

Have you heard that some people who live together for a while actually begin to look alike? More accommodation! But if they truly are going to be one, they must unite with a goal, a purpose in life designed to benefit others aside from themselves. It shouldn't just be about acquiring a house, two cars, nice furniture, extravagant vacations, or two or more children. With or without these possessions, the couple must link arms with a goal outside of themselves to benefit others—an altruistic goal to be reached.

One of the reasons that our (Ron and Nancy's) marriage has lasted and blossomed for more than 45 years is that long ago we decided that our goal was to benefit mankind; to help people to identify their wounds, and to give them the tools necessary for success in life. Our life is devoted primarily to that pursuit. While we haven't neglected each other, or our family (not that we get to spend as much time with them as we'd like), or our home, we have placed our ministry as our focus. Even working at that together was, at first, a challenge. But having accomplished that, we choose, even in semi-retirement, to continue reaching out to others.

When a couple has nothing to do but work their nine-to-five jobs, eat dinner, and watch television, they soon become annoyed and find themselves sniping at each other for no reason at all. Give that couple a purpose, a job to do for the greater good of others, and they will rise above petty annoyances, link hands, and work at blessing others. In some cases, couples who are in sync with one another actually share very similar sinus rhythms of their hearts—their hearts beat as one. We actually found that to be true in a recent physical exam by our primary care doctor.

BE INTIMATE. "They were naked and not ashamed." Here the Bible is not actually speaking about clothing because we are aware that Adam and Eve's clothing, even after they sinned, was skimpy at best—fig leaves and then animal skins.

Here the formula means that when we are to be open, vulnerable, and have nothing to hide that we will feel no shame. God designs that if two people are indeed one, they will not keep information from each other. If you are to truly understand your mate, why he or she thinks and acts as they do, why would you chose to hold back information regarding your earliest experiences? We'll tell you why many couples do hold back pertinent information. They are afraid that if they tell their history, their partner will think less of them or will reject or abandon them. *Why do they fear that?* When children are wounded, they absorb the fault, the guilt for what they received. That un-confessed guilt turns to shame in only a few days. Guilt says "I did a wrong thing," while shame says, "I am wrong. Something is deficit, no good about me." Living with that noose around one's neck predicts that *"no one will ever want to get really close to me, and if I get close to someone else, they may find out how bad I am and then leave me."*

It's amazing how victims end up carrying the shame of their perpetrators rather than assigning that shame to the rightful owner. In your mind you may assign blame and/or shame to the perpetrator, but your heart, your emotions sometimes display that you are feeling guilt and shame for what the guilty party did or neglected to do.

Many end up hiding or "stuffing their feelings," any feelings. Even feelings of happiness or pleasure are hard for some to share. Some folk have difficulty identifying what they are feeling. When they are asked how they feel, they respond with "I don't know" or "I don't feel anything." Actually, most people have feelings, but they may have been conditioned in childhood to deny them, not share them, or may have been told that feelings are irrelevant and immaterial. Those hidden feelings, while they can be confusing and often unreliable, meaning that they sometimes seem to have no basis in fact, are often the controllers of our thoughts and behaviors: *What you perceive you believe as truth*.

One way to look at it is that feelings may have very little "foundation" for their existence. However, some place back in the recesses of your mind you have a memory or the emotional punch from a memory that has created a specific feeling today. When something arises in the present, automatically, and unaware of doing so, you race through your memory bank and pull out memories or pieces of memory that match up with the current circumstance. When this happens, you will respond or react out of not just the present situation but also from the memory fragments of the past. Often this is why your reactions are more dramatic or emotional than they would be if they were based just on the current situation.

In his interesting book, *The Half-Empty Heart*, Alan Downs, Ph.D. writes: "*To help you learn the process of discriminating your feelings, remember the acronym FEEL.*"

FEEL is a simple but very powerful tool. Feel is an acronym for:

F - Feel **the feeling completely.** Name it as in, "I feel . . ." "Force yourself to give it a name."

E - Examine **the feeling.** "How much of this feeling is actually connected to what happened to me? How much of this feeling is primary—connected to the present situation—and how much is from the past? "The primary feeling is the one you want to hold onto."

E - Express **the feeling honestly.** We need others to hear us, acknowledge our Feeling, and respond to it.

L - **Let others** *validate* **your feelings.** "Perhaps the most satisfying aspect of emotions is having someone validate them. Emotional validation is important to the maintenance of relationships. Saying "I love you" between husband and wife is a critical and often overlooked exchange between couples (pp. 166 -171)

How then can you get past your unwillingness or inability to identify your feelings? You may have discovered in your childhood or even in your marriage that your parents (in childhood) or your partner (now) doesn't seem to want to hear about your feelings. That would indicate their lack of comfort with feelings, giving you a clue about their history. If this is your situation, find a counselor or friend who will listen, who will validate you and your feelings.

As you and your partner confront your histories in the process of recovery, you will learn to practice the **FEEL** technique, and will become more and more comfortable in sharing with your partner. *Start with small stuff* rather than dumping a load of hardship and misery. Perhaps talk about how you feel about hiring a babysitter to watch your children while you two have a date. Or perhaps share how you feel so special and amorous when you get to enjoy a candlelight dinner, just the two of you, alone at some special hideaway.

In one couple with whom we have worked, the wife had been sexually abused in childhood and teen years. In her several decades of marriage, she had hidden that secret from her husband; had shared it with no one, until attending one of our seminars. She questioned if she should share this with her husband, fearing that he would have great disdain for her if she did. We counseled her that no doubt the opposite would be true, that he would have greater understanding and sympathy. When she did share her secret with him, a greater understanding of and compassion for her and comprehension of their intimacy difficulties throughout the years was the result, and he even offered to accompany her for a face to face discussion with and forgiveness of her perpetrators.

Let us interject here that there are only two basic emotions. All other emotions stem from these two basic feelings. One is fear, and all negative thoughts, feelings, and behaviors come from it. The other is love, with all positive emotions, thoughts, and behaviors stemming from it. The human mind is designed to see to it that the body and mind will survive at all costs, and will develop all manner of thoughts and feelings, positive and negative, along with the corresponding behaviors, to see to it that the person will survive. Believe it or not, even the desperation of suicide is a survival technique—the choice made to not have to endure any longer the tormented thoughts and feelings and horrid experiences of life. For that person, suicide makes them survive by a final escape.

When you are going through the **FEEL** process, sharing your feelings with your mate, make sure that you have eye to eye contact. For years we have taught a seminar entitled "Marriage Enrichment." In it, couples are taught about techniques for listening and speaking, techniques for sharing their love for each other verbally, and techniques for sharing difficult thoughts and concerns. We always taught couples to sit eye to eye, and knee to knee, so that as they spoke, they could look into the "windows of the soul," the eyes, and feel that they were truly heard. Actually any subject can be broached if it is done in the context of feelings.

Let's take for example a wife whose husband is gone many hours of every day, working. She is home alone while the children are in school, and has the full responsibility of them when the school bus drops them at the door. Most meals are eaten with only her children, and routinely she fixes a plate for her husband to heat in the microwave when he does come home. Family time is basically non-existent, and many nights she crawls into bed alone.

Is she angry about him being gone so much? Of course she is, but anger is a secondary emotion. There is always a primary emotion—a source for the anger. The real truth is that she is hurt. She married her man to be with him, but he's never around. She wonders if he has fallen out of love with her, if he has another lover, if he is really out with the guys instead of at work, as he tells her he is. Her imagination runs away with her, and in her mind she conjures up all manner of "real" reasons that he isn't home.

So one night she decides to confront him about his perpetual absence. Here we already have a problem—she is going to *confront* him, and that sounds like a battle. Remember, there are only two positions: offense and defense. If she takes the offense, which it sounds like she is going to, defense is the only thing left for him. And so he defends, but before they know it, he is on the offense and she on the defense, and they are in a battle royal, accusing and blaming.

If she had chosen to simply say to him, "*Sweetheart, I am really feeling lonely for you,*" things might go a whole lot better! The point is she offers him her feeling: "I feel" . . . and then a feeling word. Not, "I feel *that . . .*" because with that preface she is about to offer an opinion or an accusation, and that's the set-up for war. However, few will argue with her statement of fact, with her statement of how she is feeling.

Very few couples know how to approach each other with this kind way to solve an issue. What they learned in childhood set them up to fight rather than to share truth and feelings. But you can learn! You can choose to share a feeling rather than to stab with an accusation.

We recall one couple in particular. They had heard us on our Boston radio program and called to make an appointment. Into our office came two young professionals, dressed beautifully and with polished deportment. After exchanging opening greetings for a couple of minutes, we asked them what pain in their lives or relationship had brought them to see us. He spoke first, telling us that they guessed they had fallen out of love with one another because they hardly even spoke. She shared the busyness of their lives, the fact they had three beautiful children, two professional careers, an expensive home in the suburbs, and two cars. By all appearances they had all that they could need or want, but had lost the reason that they were together in the first place.

We asked questions and they answered. It became evident rather quickly that they had gotten caught up in the work-a-day world, endeavoring to have exactly what the Jones' had. Having both come from divorced parents, they knew no other option than what they had learned in childhood. Somehow, listening to the radio program, they had decided to see if anything at all could be done to save what was left of a faltering marriage.

They'd come for two sessions, or maybe it was three, when we decided to teach them how to communicate. Before they left from the teaching session, we handed them a piece of paper with a list of about 25 subjects on it. These were topics for dialogue, for sharing feelings, for discussion. We had suggested that together they clean up the kitchen after supper, together they put their children to bed for the night, and then they go to their bedroom and sit cross-legged on their bed, eye to eye and knee to knee. *"Forget the television!"* we told them. *"You can catch the news on your way to work in the morning. Spend your evenings, taking one subject each night and sharing with each other your true feelings."* At first, they thought we were crazy, but they agreed to follow instructions and do their homework. Their next appointment was scheduled for a week later.

When they came to the office the following week, they were beaming. *"We just love dialoging"* they exclaimed. *"Each night we can hardly wait to get the children's baths done and stories read, so we can go to our room to talk. It feels almost like we are dating again, and we have rediscovered each other in a way we never had before."* We had two more sessions for answering their questions and making sure that they were still dialoguing, and they were "good to go."

Certainly not all couples are on the road to healing that quickly. Many have deep issues that they have let simmer on some back burner of their minds for a long time, letting the pot of resentment get fuller with each passing day. And as it does, the lid of the pot begins to dance with the increasing heat, and finally, like a pressure cooker gone amuck, they blow.

Unfortunately, many couples do this. Women especially seem to burn slower and hold onto perceived or actual injustices longer. Rather than seeking help or sharing their angst with their husbands, they simmer until they can no longer handle the pressure. All too often, when the marriage begins to explode, the woman has gone past her boiling-over point, and has decided that it's too late to repair the situation. Hopefully, the fact that you are reading this book means that you are still hopeful, that you are still looking for answers to your relationship. All too many couples divorce before they seek help, and then after the divorce they wish they had asked for help before jumping into the divorce court.

So the formula, with its four pieces, forms a circle, a sacred circle. So long as all components are adhered to, a perfect circle is formed—a sacred circle. If the first ingredient, LEAVE, is not taken seriously and practiced, then automatically someone(s) other than your mate are in your marriage, and perhaps you are in theirs. If the second piece, CLEAVE, is not practiced, then there is definitely someone else in your marriage, that someone who you could just not leave behind, someone with whom

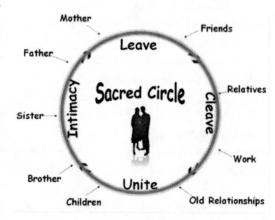

you have chosen to place primary allegiance. Your ability to glue in a permanent non-wavering bond is sacrificed. If the second piece, UNITE, is ignored, then not only will your marriage be without sexual pleasure, but it will also be without a higher purpose. Rather than looking outside of yourselves to bless others, you will be "naval-gazing," seeking to satisfy the emptiness you feel with bigger and better "things." You will attach yourself to objects rather than to your mate. And finally, if you are not intimate (in-to-me-see) with each other, then you will live as married singles, occupying the same house and perhaps even the same bed, but will live two separate lives.

Miss one piece of the pie, and there will be space and opportunity for the "Sacred Circle" of your marriage to be compromised or maybe invaded by a third or fourth party. Around each couple there should be an unbroken Sacred Circle. Into this circle, no other human being has the right to enter, unless the couple is seeking aid to repair a wounded part of their relationship and have decided to take a counselor into their confidence. The amazing thing is that most couples who have a complete Sacred Circle, will not need marriage counseling. They will be able to solve

most hurdles that arise between them because they are "naked and not ashamed."

It is always the duty of the **man** to do the departing from his parents when he marries. Even after years of marriage, this issue can be eliminated – look at the following story of Charlie and Candie . . .

All of his life, Charlie had been his mother's pet, and Charlie's father had felt like he was the fifth wheel, certainly out of the family's loop. Even after Charlie married, his mother kept very close tabs on him and not only ignored, but was unkind to his wife. It had come to the point that Candie threatened, *"It's either me or your mother. You decide."* Charlie was in a panic. He loved his wife dearly and could not even think of losing her, but how in the world could he detach from his mother without wounding *her*?

They presented this situation to us at a seminar. *"They're about to celebrate their fortieth wedding anniversary by taking a trip to Hawaii,"* Charlie said, *"but I doubt they even have a relationship!"*

We asked Charlie if he knew when they were flying to Hawaii, what day, what time, what airline? Of course he did. We made this suggestion: Write a letter to your parents. Apologize to them for taking a position in their marriage that you shouldn't have. Tell your father that you're sorry for taking his place with your mother. Tell your mother that you're giving her husband back to her. No longer will you be chatting on the phone with her every day, sharing your marriage with her. Make it a kind and loving letter to them both. Enclose the letter in a sealed envelope. The day of the flight, go to a florist and buy the most extravagant orchid corsage you can get and a beautiful boutonniere for your father. Then go to the airport and surprise them. Pin the corsage on your mother and the flower on your dad's lapel. Then give them the envelope with the letter you've enclosed, and tell them they can't open it until they're airborne.

Then we asked, *"Can you do this?"*

"I surely can, and I will!" he responded excitedly.

Charlie made it to the airport with a letter and the flowers, and shocked his parents before their departure. Has it made a difference, you ask? Most definitely! Has his and Candie's marriage been saved? Yes it has, and since that time they have two lovely children, a new house, and a beautiful life together.

If the husband will do his work, will recover from his parental attachment wound from Mother, the wife will respond, and with help their marriage can quickly be healed. WHY? What has happened? Because he no longer feels pressured and his loyalty is no longer divided between the two women in his life. There is no question, his wife is Number one!

God's formula for marriage—LEAVE, CLEAVE, UNITE, and BE INTIMATE—*always* works when we understand its full meaning and adhere to its principles. If both husband and wife will do personal recovery and be willing to "leave your father's house" and work through the memories of events for which forgiveness is required, both will be able to move on, to relate well with each other and with their God. God will be in the center of their Sacred Circle, not as an invader but as the actual glue who holds you them both together as one.

IN SUMMARY:

God offered the formula for marital success in the Garden of Eden to Adam and Eve. It is recorded in Genesis 2:24 and 25. When couples understand the true meaning of the words, and are willing to adhere to God's instruction, their marriage will be a sacred circle, into which no other person or enterprise will enter. The couple will be in complete harmony with each other, have the ability to work through any feelings that arise and are open and honest with each other about history, current life, and feelings. Learning the proper way to share feelings with each other, with one goal and purpose, a couple is guaranteed that any hurdle can be surmounted, as hand in hand they are a benefit to their children and to society.

LEAVE, CLEAVE, UNITE and BE INTIMATE—God's formula for success.

Questions for You to Answer and Share

1. When you came to the relationship with your mate, what baggage did you bring with you?

2. Is what you learned in childhood from your parents helping or hurting your relationship?

   • How?

3. How did you learn to solve conflict? What method do you use to solve conflict today in your relationship?

CHAPTER NINE

Heart to Heart

Brains are designed for survival; hearts are designed for love. You've read that before, right? But now we are going to expand upon that information so that you can learn the importance of marital happiness being found not just on a social, intellectual, or sexual basis, but on the connection between two hearts.

Think about this . . . Point to the area on your body where you add up all the positives about your sweetheart. Now point to the area of your body where you express your love for him or her. You *think* in your brain, don't you? And you *love* in your heart! You wouldn't point to your brain when you would speak about your love for your mate.

How we begin . . .

Before we are born our DNA contains specific instructions about how our bodies and brains are formed. Our brain structure is designed to develop and live in a particular environment, one that will supply our needs during specific windows of opportunity, so that we will be emotionally and physically healthy. We are designed with five specific objectives to be accomplished. They are:

- **Safety.** The structure at the base of the brain (the brain stem) is designed for survival, is prepared for emergencies, and it desires safety—the need to be free from having to run, to fight, to freeze, or to submit.

- **Belonging or Reliable Membership.** We are designed to live in community, not alone. It is about coming together, staying together, and attaching and forming secure attachments. This is a hardwired attribute of the brain, located in the midbrain, and is not an option.

- **Diversity or Difference.** This is formed in the upper brain, the cortex and this objective is complex and variable. When children come to understand that each person sees or perceives differently, it often creates fear in them. They need to seek comfort for what they learn about being different from others, especially their parents. Because of this, children seek safe and reliable relationships where they sense that it's OK to be different.

- **Autonomy.** The ability to choose. The upper brain has the ability to choose between alternatives, between experiences and actions. As humans we observe, process what we observe, and choose actions, and sometimes all this takes place in a split second. We always take previous experience into account when we are determining an action. We are hardwired to choose a community or relationships that let us make decisions.

- **Purpose.** Having purpose leads us into a spiritual realm, and is located in the frontal cortex. Every person is born with a gift, a potential. When we live it we are productive and a blessing to others in our community, we feel a sense of purpose, of accomplishment, and a reason for living. This purpose-living is hardwired for us to seek community and companionship that will nurture us and need us.

Dr. Paul Pearsall, a world famous psycho-neuro-immunologist who studies the *correlation* between the workings of the mind, the nervous system, and health to the body, states in his book, *The Heart's Code:*

"In its potentially lethal covenant with its body, the brain never shuts up. It is designed to constantly be on some level of alert. Even as you dream, it tries to get your attention. It is in a state of perpetual readiness to react, defend or react when it or its body senses threats – real or not—to its self-enhancement. The brain itself never truly falls completely asleep. It has different levels of vigilance, but it never gives up its hold on the body. The brain-body covenant is

one designed primarily for staying alive, seeking stimulation, doing and getting. In effect, your brain 'drags' your body with it to do its bidding, hauling you and your heart along on its rough ride, whether or not you are sure 'in your heart' that you want to go where it is taking you" (p. 24).

Continuing on, Pearsall writes: *"The brain is afraid of cognitive darkness. It constantly seeks input and feeds on new, different, intense stimulation. For the brain, old news is no news at all. Like a child waking in a night terror, it often jolts you back to its form of reality from a peaceful, brief reverie. It resists beauty that 'arrests' its attention from self-survival. Its primary value is self-health not splendor, going and not being, and grit rather than grace"* (p. 25).

Some facts he offers about the brain are:

- It is programmed to seek success, not connection,
- The brain is an ultimate "Type A."
- It is always in a hurry, preparing its body to go somewhere.
- It is uncomfortable with "just being" anywhere (p. 25).

Now Consider this:

While the human brain, a three-pound universe, is fearfully and wonderfully made and designed to see that we survive, the human heart is designed to pump life-giving blood throughout the body, to offer optimal health to the organs and cells, and to offer life-giving love, seeing to it that we thrive.

The heart is the very first organ to develop while we are in the womb, beginning to beat 18 to 22 days after conception, in most cases before a woman even knows she is pregnant. One of the first things an obstetrician will do on a woman's first exam is to use a Doppler, applied to the lower abdomen to amplify the sound of the fetus's heartbeat.

The heart is the first responder to external stimuli, and holds emotional memory of experiences, even while still in the womb. It connects with the brain via the vagus nerve, and it is designed to work in harmony with the brain.

"The vagus nerve, also called pneumogastric nerve, cranial nerve X, the Wanderer or sometimes the Rambler, is the tenth of twelve (excluding CN0) paired cranial nerves. Upon leaving the medulla (brain stem) it extends through the jugular foramen, then passing into the carotid sheath between the internal carotid artery and the internal jugular vein down below the head, to the neck, chest and abdomen, where it contributes to the innervation of the viscera (the trunk of the body containing our organs). Besides output to the various organs in the body the vagus nerve conveys sensory information about the state of the body's organs to the central nervous system. 80-90% of the nerve fibers in the vagus nerve are afferent (sensory) nerves communicating the state of the viscera to the brain" ("Functional and chemical anatomy of the afferent vagal system," Berthoud HR and Neuhuber WL). The heart and the brain are supposed to be team players, but external forces often sabotage the functioning of the connection between the two. This is often set up during the third trimester of pregnancy and is due to the relationship the mother has with the man who impregnated her. Some scientists are convinced that experiences of neglect, abuse, loss, and emotional disconnection can disrupt the working relationship between heart and brain, causing many to live totally out of the survival brain – in survival mode, living in fear.

Dr. Pearsall contrasts the heart to the brain, the heart . . .

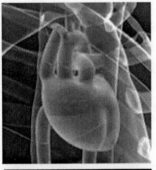

- "Thinks more in a "Type B," gentle, relaxed and connective way."
- "Searches to connect its 'L' energy with other hearts to establish lasting relationships and intimacy."

"The brain seems to WANT to have a 'blast,' while the heart NEEDS to have a 'bond'" (*The Heart's Code*, p. 25).

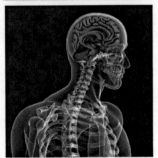

He contrasts brain and heart by referring to the brain as "*selfish*" and to the heart as "*altruistic*" (*Ibid.* p, 26).

The heart seeks to connect, to reach out to others, to be part of a greater community.

In 1979, a secret study was reported by Stewart Wolf and John G. Bruhn. It was titled

"Roseta Story: An Anatomy of Health," and published by the University of Oklahoma Press. Dr Stewart Wolf, a physician, and John G, Bruhn, a sociologist, had made a long-term study of the inhabitants of Roseto, Pennsylvania, from 1935 to 1984. Dr. Mimi Guarneri reports on that study in her fascinating book, *The Heart Speaks*.

"Despite the community's smoking, eating a fatty diet, and spending their days in the hazardous labor of slate quarries, the citizens of Roseto, the researchers discovered, appeared to be almost immune to heart disease, dying at a rate only half that of the rest of the country.

"Roseto's early Italian immigrants had built their own culture of cooperation, after being ostracized by the Welsh and English, who'd once dominated their small area of Eastern Pennsylvania. They created a kind of civil spirit, celebrating religious festivals and family occasions together, evolving into an intensely connected community.

"In Roseto, . . . neighbors looked after one another, generations lived together under a single roof, and the elderly were included as part of a close-knit web. Church festivals, social clubs and family dinners brought people together and served to ward off isolation and loneliness."

"Through the 1960's, Roseto was characterized by stability, predictability and conformity. Families lived in small homes on tightly packed streets; neighbors often filled one another's kitchens after dinner. Since any display of wealth was discouraged, the distance between rich and poor was diminished. The work ethic was paramount: A common goal shared by nearly everyone was a better future for their children."

"In the end the researchers decided that the Roseto Effect on heart disease was caused by something that couldn't be measured in a lab—social networks, civic interconnectedness, stability and predictability" (pp. 8, 9).

What this does is to simply emphasize the importance of connectedness, or relationship between people. Since the heart is designed to connect, doing so made it healthy.

However, when the next generation came along, in the 1970's things began to reverse. Younger townspeople bought cars and took white collar jobs out of town. They fenced in their single-family houses built on the outskirts of town, and their health began to deteriorate. The first heart attack of a person under age 45 was reported in 1971. The rate of heart disease continued to rise until it reached the national average. How sad!

Continuing further in *The Heart Speaks*, Dr. Guaneri reports that studies done for a period of five to nine years in Alameda County, California, and in Finland concluded that "socially isolated participants demonstrated a two- to threefold increased risk of death from heart disease and all other causes. Strikingly, these results were independent of other cardiac risk factors" (p. 9).

While your heart belongs to you, it is a social organ. It loves to connect, and thrives when doing so, as long as the connection is positive. The electromagnetic current of the heart is 60 times higher in amplitude than is the field of the brain. It has the ability to send energy fields that are 5,000 times stronger than the energy field of the brain. It is measured from four- and one-half to ten feet from the body, with differing measurements for different people.

According to cardiologist, Mimi Guarneri, "The heart is also exquisitely sensitive to emotions. An angry or fearful thought changes the heart-rate variability (HRV) pattern—the beat-to- beat variability between each heartbeat—which sets the pace for the brain and the respiratory system" (p. 158).

According to HeartMath Institute in Boulder Creek, California, who have been studying the heart and heart-brain functioning for a number of years, recurring stress patterns are difficult to break using the mind alone. That's why techniques that focus on the power of the heart rather than on the power of the brain alone, are frequently successful. A key finding of the HeartMath Institute is that when 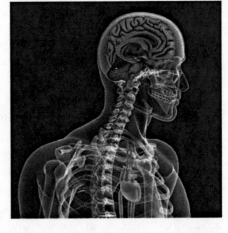 people learn to maintain heart-focused positive states of feeling, the brain is brought into "entrainment" or coherence with the heart. Both organs, working in tandem, in cooperation with each other create the healthiest physical conditions in the body and emotional peace.

Connecting Hearts . . .

The human heart is designed to pump life-giving blood throughout the body, to be sure, but beyond that physiological function it is designed to make the most intimate connections possible. It is designed to hold emotional memory for future reference, as it was recorded by Moses speaking to the Children of Israel before they crossed, without him, over the River Jordan to the promised Canaan land. He admonished the people that if they did not keep God's commands, He would scatter them among the peoples of other nations, and only a few would survive. But Moses also promised them that even in the land of idolaters, if they "would seek the Lord your God, you will find Him if you look for him with all your heart and with all your soul" (Deut. 4:29). If they would seek with all their emotions and the memories contained in their hearts of His loving mercies to them in the past, they would find Him, connect with Him.

In the book of Deuteronomy there are six other references to "loving God with all the *heart*." "Serve the Lord with all your *heart*," (Joshua 22:5), "' . . . the Lord looks at the *heart*'" (1 Sam. 16:7). 1 Chronicles 28:9 states that "the Lord searches every *heart*".

Repeatedly in Scripture the heart is referred to in many contexts. We have always thought that the Greek word "cardia" and the Hebrew word "leb," the original language words used for heart, referred to the mind. But it appears that this is not always the case.

In Psalm 86:11, David asks God for an undivided *heart* so that he can fear God's name. In Psalm 139:23, he asks God to search him and know his *heart*. Proverbs 27:19 states that "a man's *heart* reflects the man."

According to biblical scholar Spiros Zodhiates, compiled from Strong's Lexicon, "*In the Bible, the whole spectrum of human emotions is attributed to the (physical) heart. There are many Hebrew idioms which are built with "leb."*

"*Wisdom and understanding reside in the heart,*" (1 Kings 3:12; Prov. 16:23). "*To refuse to make a proper decision is to harden the heart,*" (Ex. 10:1 and Joshua 11:20). "*The heart is the seat of moral evil*" (Eccl. 9:3).

Scripture tells us that God's dwelling place during Israel's wanderings in the wilderness was in the special compartment of the Tabernacle known as the Holy of Holies. In the Old Testament (Jer. 31:33) and the New Testament (Heb. 10:16) God promises to make a new covenant with Israel (that's us). He promised to move the Law from the physical Tabernacle to the physical body: "*I will write my laws on their hearts,*" He says. Could it be that the heart where God's law is now written is, in fact, the Holy of Holies, God's dwelling place?

Remember the story of the time before Christ's death when Jesus was comforting His disciples? It's found in John 14:22, 23. Judas (not Judas Iscariot) asked Him, "But, Lord, why do you intend to show yourself to us and not to the world?" Jesus replied, "If anyone loves me, he will obey my teaching. My father will love him, and we will come to him and make our home with him."

Jesus made this promise to His disciples, and if we are unguarded to receiving and loving God, our hearts, our bodies, can become sanctuaries, the dwelling place of the divine. Paul states it well in Galatians 2:20: *"I have been crucified with Christ, and I no longer live, but Christ lives in me."* We have definitely connected!

The heart longs to connect, but in order to do so, we must connect with *it*. We must be willing to give up the brain's need to control ourselves and others. When we do, the wall that we have constructed, blocking access between the heart and mind, will crumble. Actually the "taking down of the wall" is not accomplished like it was in East Berlin, by men and machinery, but it is taken down brick by brick, memory by memory, negative emotion upon negative emotion, as we resolve the issues of the past that have caused us to think we were surviving by constructing it.

"The Journey inward is aptly described by its title, for it is a deep and very personal inward journey. It almost always comes as an unsettling experience, yet results in healing for those who continue through it. It is a time when the issues primarily go up and down between you and God. Others are involved, but the focus is on the issues, battle, healing and resolution in your relationship with God" (*The Critical Journey*, p. 93).

We know that you want to improve your relationship with your mate, that's why you're reading this book, answering the questions, and learning more about yourself and your mate than you ever thought possible. But the key is this: heart to heart relationships are spiritual. They involve the prefrontal cortex of the brain where decision-making, moral values, and spirituality are contained, and to be whole and healthy they must involve the "L" energy, the LOVE of the heart as well. To insure success in intimate relationships, cooperation between the heart and the brain is necessary. In order for the brain and the heart to cooperate, the brain must give up its determination for getting and doing, and submit to the giving and being of the heart. You must be willing to take down those protective bricks and allow the light of love to penetrate.

Nancy: After twelve years of marriage the wall erected between us had grown so large that we could no longer see over it or peek through it to find each other. Our marriage was coming to an end.

Ron: God directed me to return to school. At the time, I had no idea that it would save our marriage. My thought was that I get out of pastoral ministry and into another career. I would become a Marriage and Family Therapist—to prepare for my divorce. Somehow I reasoned that even if I couldn't seem to save my marriage, maybe I could fix everyone else's. Ridiculous, don't you think? But God had a different plan.

Nancy: After sitting through his first class Ron came home and demanded that I change my clothes and *"get in the car."* We headed to Boston, *"to get you enrolled,"* Ron told me, *"because if I learn all this, we definitely will be in different places and our marriage won't survive."*

And so we learned together. We looked at our beginnings, and began to examine each brick, to work through the reason it had been cemented into the dividing wall, and to use it as a stepping stone to emotional health and heart-to-heart connection. As each issue was raised, our hearts began to open to let each other in. Becoming aware of the junk that had separated us, the pain that each of us had experienced in the years of childhood and adolescence, the acceptance we both longed for began to appear.

Nancy: Finally Ron could begin to accept that I did, in fact, love him. He felt it in his chest. I began to trust the man I married more than the man who had conceived me. I no longer looked for Ron to fill the emptiness that had been left by my emotionally distant relationship with my father; that issue had been dealt with, forgiven, and released. On the other hand, Ron no longer expected me to fill his mother-emptiness, left behind from conception, from attempted abortion, from abandonment and neglect. That issue had been dealt with, face-to-face, before her death."

Of course we reviewed our marital years and the various hurts we had felt in our relationship. Forgiveness came easy because we were now aware of the "stuff" that each had brought to the marriage; we saw how we'd been set up for our dysfunction. Suddenly, we understood each other.

Forgiveness is not simply the exchange of the words, *"I am sorry. Please forgive me,"* nor is it the reply, *"I forgive you."* Forgiveness is not something that we as humans muster up. It is a gift from God that we either accept or refuse. If we accept it, we pass it on to others. If we can experience God's forgiveness of us, that gift of love and acceptance He offers has a path available to flow out from us to others.

As you continue in your path—the way of loosening your brain's hold on you, its need to do, to go, and to survive—your heart begins to relax, to enjoy the stress-less environment, to revel in its new ability to connect. As you feel the pain carried by your mate, because you have become safe for him or her to share it with you, as you offer words of comfort, you will feel your heart open wide. It will be as if a key had turned in its lock and the heart gates gradually open to usher you across a bridge from self-centeredness and out of coherence or harmony to other-centeredness, altruism.

With your old baggage of resentment, anger, fear, and sadness gone, you are a fit vessel in which God's spirit can dwell. That spirit will reach out to your mate, enfold them with God's love, and the two hearts shall beat as one. This is who you were designed to be as a couple. This is your spiritually intimate destination.

Questions for You to Answer and Share

1. What is the most interesting information you learned about the human heart in this chapter?

    Why is this so interesting to you?

2. If you were asked to give <u>evidence</u> that you live from either your head (brain) in survival mode or from your heart (love mode), what would you say?

3. What would be frightening about opening your heart and being emotionally vulnerable with your mate?

CHAPTER TEN

It's Just the Beginning

Today is September 23, and as we write, the computer sits on a tray table in the first class cabin on a flight to Milwaukee, Wisconsin. We are grateful for these seats, as they afford us the room and comfort to write. Today's trip to Milwaukee is not at all like the trip we each took 46 years ago. Then, unknown to us both, we would meet the love of our lives. Now we are going there (thankfully, not in a blizzard) to say good-bye to Phyllis's husband Johnny. (You'll remember that Phyllis is Ron's older sister, the one who often cared for him when he was a baby.) Johnny is struggling to breathe and fighting a nasty infection in his leg that has a 25-year-old knee replacement. Somehow the screws in his replacement have come loose, and caused this infection, invading his entire leg. He can no longer walk.

Johnny and Phyllis have been married for well over 50 years. Theirs has been a marriage of cooperation, raising their four children, and both working to provide adequately for their family. John worked long hours at a hard job and Phyllis, in order to stay home with her children, took in ironing to do for other families, spending hours standing behind her rickety ironing board. Often when John was home from work and dinner was over, he would do the dishes while Phyllis got the children to bed. And then he would help her to iron. They were a team with twin irons and ironing boards, working lovingly together to beyond exhaustion, but doing what was right for their family. They were team players.

126

Regularly they attended their neighborhood Catholic Church and saw to it that their children received a religious education, but they chose to not wear their religion on their sleeves. Yet they lived it in every way possible, following the Golden Rule of doing unto others what they would like others to do for them. In 1957, Phyllis's (and Ron's) father suddenly died of a massive heart attack. Ron was just 16, and had two younger siblings. His parents had moved to Arkansas for Mother's health, but money was scarce, causing stress to Ron's dad. Perhaps the added stress was one of the causes of his heart attack at age 50.

The move back to Milwaukee was traumatic to say the least, and Ron's mother, totally overcome with grief, was unable to function. As a result, Phyllis and Johnny willingly took her and the three children into their home. Quickly they finished two upstairs rooms, giving enough space for four new family members, and adding both physical and financial burden to their young family. The four lived with Phyl and John for two years, until Mother "got on her feet" enough to get a job, save enough to rent an apartment, and take her children to a place of their own. It was during this time, that Ron left home and joined the Navy. Whatever needed to be done for the family, John and Phyllis willingly did; no complaints, no whining, just lovingly doing.

That first year that her parents and the kids had moved to Arkansas, in a phone conversation Phyl's mother told her that there wouldn't be a Christmas for the children that year. There just wasn't enough money for it, as the move had taken all their reserve. So Phyllis and Johnny went to a loan company and borrowed enough money to make a decent Christmas for Phyl's younger siblings, and wired the money to Arkansas. They spent the next year paying off that loan. The very next winter, Johnny's mother was about to have her gas turned off because she was three months in arrears on her bill. There would be no surviving a Milwaukee winter with no heat, so again, John and Phyllis went to the loan company. They borrowed enough money to pay her gas bill plus several months in advance, so John's mother could be warm.

In 1964, Ron's younger brother, Bobby, left his mother's home and joined the army. That meant that the Social Security money Mother was receiving for Bobby, stopped coming in. April of 1965, youngest sibling, Judy married. Again, Mother lost the income she was receiving for Judy, creating another financial crisis. The meager wage that mother earned from her job in a bakery was not adequate to support her large apartment, pay the utilities, and buy groceries. So John and Phyl suggested that she move in with them, rather than them having to take loans to supplement her income.

For 20 years, until her death in 1987, Ron's mother lived with Phyllis and John. She worked until her legs would not allow her to stand for long periods, and then retired. Sometimes she came to our home in New England, staying with us for three to six months at a time, giving Phyl and John a break. But the majority of her time was spent in Phyl and Johnny's home. Family was close by, and often they gathered at Phyllis's home for family meals in the backyard or in the refurbished basement that had been designed for large family parties. Fun and laughter often filled their home.

In all of this hard work and doing for others, John and Phyl always took time for themselves as a couple. Money was scarce, so they spent little on themselves, but would go to a theater where movies were affordable, buy a bag of popcorn to share, and just be happy holding hands and being together. When they bought groceries, they did it together whenever they could. Time just for the two of them was always important, and that helped to keep the spark of romance in their marriage, even when times were tough.

Finally the time came for John to retire. He left the company he had worked for with a pension and social security and that gave them enough to enjoy their Golden years together. With their children grown, educated, and married, and Ron's mother deceased, they decided to buy a little place in the warm climate of Florida. A doublewide in a senior park was just the ticket. After selling their place in Milwaukee, they packed their belongings and headed for their dream home. In that senior park, they had a ball! They rode bicycles, played bingo a couple of times a week, visited with friends, went to a one-dollar movie once a week, and occasionally out to a local restaurant for breakfast. In the evening they got together with friends, played games, and sipped iced tea. One little family at a time, their children and grandchildren would come to visit, staying in the home's guest room, enjoying Disneyland, the beaches, and being together with Mom and Dad.

But shortly after their move to Florida, the company where John had worked for a lifetime was sold and his retirement was lost. No real explanations came with the shocking news, just that his retirement income would not be transferred. That cut their income substantially, but John and Phyl made do with Social Security. There were always inexpensive things they could do to make ends meet while still enjoying their life together. They would enjoy each day to the fullest, remaining best friends throughout their years.

Early in our ministry, we learned a lesson, a lesson we've never forgotten, from a couple in our first district. We had moved on to our second district after nearly five years. One day we received a call telling us of the impending death of a woman in our previous district who had been an especially dear friend. Bernice was a life-long schoolteacher, wife, and mother. She and her husband John lived in a beautiful home overlooking a lake. We had visited there numerous times, taking our daughters with us, because they loved to prance around in Bernice's high-heeled shoes while wearing one of her mink stoles. Occasionally she'd bake a luscious maple cake just because Ron loved them.

We arrived at her hospital bedside to find our friend near death. John had told us that we could talk to her, "*but she won't know you,*" he said. Ron took her hand and bent over, kissing her forehead. "*Do you know who kissed you?*" John asked. "*Oh yes, that's my pastor,*" she replied. Then John bent over and kissed her cheek. "*Now do you know who kissed you?*" he asked. "No," she answered, devastating poor John. We stayed a couple of hours, loving her and praying with her and John, and then drove the four hours home.

Two days passed and we were called again; this time to perform her funeral. As has always been Ron's custom, we would stand by the coffin while, after the services, attendees passed by to pay respects one last time. All the guests had left except for John. He approached the casket, tears pouring down his cheeks, and asked through his sobs, "*Pastor, how am I to say good-bye to a woman I never said hello to?*" We were devastated by the question, and have never forgotten it. After more than 50 years of marriage, this couple really did not know one another. Two professionals with two professional sons, a beautiful home, and all the money they would ever need, but a relationship that was more like married singles living together, than a well-connected couple. No heart-to-heart connection.

Nancy: Many times that memory has surfaced through the years. Actually it was shortly after that funeral that Ron started graduate school for a degree in Marriage and Family Therapy, and dragged me with him to the second class. The professor stood behind her podium and announced that there were 84 students in that class, *Emotional Growth of the Family*, and one married couple. She looked directly at us and said, "*Chances are very good that your marriage will not survive this class. But if you do last, you'll be cemented for life!*"

I leaned over to Ron and whispered, "*Can we leave now?*"

"*Make it or break it, Baby*," he replied.

We were to be in both our marriage and in graduate school until the end, whatever that end looked like.

Ron: Perhaps one of the experiences that kept us working toward repairing our fractured marriage also occurred in our first parish. Jan, one of our church members was a former top model, a beautiful woman, only 32 years old. Her husband, an airline pilot, was not a church member, but always "Johnny-on-the-spot" to be of help when needed at the church. Jan was diagnosed with a rare form of liver cancer and had to go back and forth to Sloan-Kettering Hospital in New York City for treatment. They lived in a lovely Connecticut suburban home, had two beautiful daughters, and life was too enjoyable for such a horrific diagnosis and a devastating prognosis.

How Jim and Jan adored each other! As days and weeks past, Jan grew weaker, thinner, and hope waned that she would recover. Her treatments, although aggressive and cutting edge, were not helping. Her body was racked with pain, and to tolerate it and even have a wee bit of energy to communicate with their girls and her family, Jan lived on morphine and grape juice.

Jim took a leave of absence to be with her. How very lovingly he cared for her. Their master bath included a sunken tub, and each day, sometimes twice a day, he would carry her to the tub and immerse her in comforting warm water. Then he would gently bathe her, dry and powder her, put her in one of her pretty nighties, and place her back in their bed. His caring was far beyond what most nurses would do. She would lie in their bed, comforted by the warmth of his body, cradled in his arms.

Until her last moments of life, on a Friday night as the sun was setting in a golden orange sky, he spoke his love of her, whispering in her ear. Jim always said he was an atheist, but on that Friday eve, he bent down and fulfilling her greatest wish, whispered, "*I believe Jan, I believe.*" It was as if she was waiting for those words, and as he kissed her over and over again, she breathed her last. We witnessed that scene. How could we ever forget such sacrificial love?

Meanwhile, we deal with another couple, "committed Christians," married 30-somethng years, who, for the past ten years, have been on a collision course for separation and divorce. Our hearts literally hurt because it is so hard to comprehend how a beautiful couple, with talents and abilities that blend as a powerful tool for good in the world, can drift so far apart. It makes one ask if they were really together in the first place or if their marriage was more a business arrangement than a heart-to-heart connection. If they had been connected, how could a heart harden to the state that it absolutely refuses all attempts at softening or connecting? So many couples exist under the same roof and even in the same bed, but the only time they touch is if, quite by accident, one foot happens to graze the other's during sleep. Granted, some couples have the sad misfortune for one or the other to drift away into dementia or Alzheimer's disease, but aside from that catastrophic outcome, how can a heart become so distanced, so hardened?

How could it be that an avowed atheist would submit to the calling of his heart and the "committed Christian" be so stuck on selfishness and self-survival? Could it be that the heart and mind have so separated that the love of the heart has ceased to exist while the mind screams, "*Protect me, save me, I want, I need? I don't care what happens to you. I just want what I want when I want it. And no matter how much you try, I will sabotage you at every turn, because I am convinced that you are my enemy, and I must protect myself.*"

In Romans, Chapter 2, verses 12 through 16 (Amplified version), are recorded these words:

"*All who have sinned without the law will also perish without the law, and all who have sinned under the law will be judged by the law. For it is not the hearers of the law who are righteous before God, but the doers of the law who will be justified. When Gentiles who have not the law do by nature what the law requires, they are a law to themselves, even though they do not have the law. They show that what the law requires is written on their hearts, while their conscience also bears witness and their conflicting thoughts accuse or perhaps excuse them on that day when, according to my Gospel, God judges the secrets of men by Christ Jesus.*"

Forgiveness does not even come into play here, for the hardened heart it is not an option. Considering that forgiveness is a gift from God and we have to be willing to receive it, it appears that the hardened heart thumbs its nose at God so to speak, refusing the very gift that would set it free. Forgiveness requires a letting go of bitterness and resentment, and the mind fears letting that go. Those negative feelings have become its wall of protection, its suit of armor. Of course, while it is in this protect mode, hidden behind cold steel, it lets no one in for comfort, except if someone might fill some self-centered temporary need. The heart is well-protected, away from the warmth of acceptance. Perhaps the following text explains:

"To set the mind on the flesh is death, but to set the mind on the Spirit is life and peace. For the mind that is set on the flesh is hostile to God; it does not submit to God's law, indeed it cannot; and those who are in the flesh cannot please God" (Rom. 8:5-8, RSV).

For a week now, Phyllis has been with John in the Health and Rehabilitation Center. She sits beside him, chats as he slips in and out of awareness, and endeavors to anticipate his every need. She feeds him what he'll eat—three spoonfuls of chicken noodle soup and a few of chocolate pudding. She worries if he's uncomfortable, if he'll slip off his chair, if he's sleeping too much, if he's in pain, or if he'll improve enough to go home.

They have been staying at their daughter Chis's home in greater Milwaukee, back from Florida so that family can watch over them. Phyl is now at John's side every moment of the day and night. For her there's no leaving the man she loves, unless her daughter can be there long enough for her to shower, wash her hair, and maybe get a few hours of sleep before she "dresses pretty for John." When she returns and John sees her with her hair fixed, and in different clothes, he whispers, "Pretty, Honey."

Phyllis has been really ill too. She has just come through cancer surgery and therapy. As she sits with John, her feet swell bigger and bigger by the hour. Only slippers will fit them as they balloon. To her it's a small price to pay to be with her John.

She asks, "Do you think he'll be able to come home soon?" Her heart longs for just a bit more time together, while at the same time she knows he can't last like he is for much longer. While she hates watching him struggle to breathe, she prays that he'll improve. He is 85 years old, with congestive heart failure, chronic obstructive pulmonary disease, mild pneumonia and a nasty infection. He's taken from chair to bed, and back again, by Hoyer Lift, because he can't even stand to pivot. Every move is a painful struggle.

We stay with them in the room and watch his breathing become shallow, his feet swell, his energy drain, and lucidness much less frequent. We picture old scenes when we were all together laughing and having fun; just being family. Oh, to return there!

It's not easy to say good-bye to family whom we have loved and who have loved us through the years, not today, and not when John takes his last breathe. However the love we've always experienced, and the love now, is part of the sorrow we experience at the very end, and we'll get through it. So will Phyllis. She's a strong and good woman, and God and family will hold her up.

The wonderful movie *Shadowlands*, tells the true story of Christian author, C.S. Lewis, recently best known for his *Narnia* series. Lewis married rather late in life for the first time, to a beautiful and intelligent woman. Soon after their marriage, it was discovered she had cancer. Her disease was already rather advanced and it soon became evident that their time together was limited. While they were on a short trip Joy broached the subject of her death. Lewis didn't want to talk about it; he'd rather pretend it wasn't in the near future. She persisted.

"The joy now is part of the pain then," she told him. While the joy in the present might be great, one cannot ignore and discount the inevitable. Sometimes, like Lewis did, we have to tell the ones we love most that it's OK to give up. We have to give them permission to let go.

How much better it is to experience loss with pleasant memories instead of with regrets of words unsaid or kind deeds undone. How much better to spend your years together really connected heart to heart. How awesome to open completely to another, hiding nothing, sharing thoughts, feelings, and love for each other. When that connection is a reality, times of illness, the coming of old age, and physical deterioration do not pose the threat or even the idea of separation. When the two have become one in heart, death only separates them physically. The partner who remains carries within him or her, the love and adoration, the memories positive and negative of the years they enjoyed together. Every misdeed has been forgiven and let go. While those memories may not fill the touch of the hand not held or provide comfort in the bed made cold and lonely by loss, the heart remains filled with love and the mind with connected, joy-filled recollections, rather than with guilt and regret.

How can you ensure that the experiences and memories that you make in your marriage are those that will hold you up when the time of loss comes? What are the ways that you can ensure the best years of marriage possible? How can you be sure that you and your mate will have a strong heart-to-heart connection – one that will last to the good-bye of death?

IN SUMMARY...

- **Start this very minute!** Wherever you are, whatever your partner is doing, STOP! Think for a minute or two about what you've read. Allow God to open your heart to your mate, and then speak the truth as only He can give it to you. You do not get the kind of love you desire by generating it within yourself. That Agape (unconditional) love comes from God, and He longs to instill it in you. Yes, He wants you to love yourself, because it is with that same love He gives you that you will love your partner, your parents, your children, and others. Any time that love has the face of selfishness on it, loves in order to receive love, says "I love you," looking for a response in kind, it is not God's perfect love . Rather, it is selfish human love, giving in order to get.

- **Apologize for your part in the pain you're both experiencing.** Take responsibility. No "buts," no "if only," no "if only you had," just pure, "I want to be an instrument for change in our relationship. Can you accept God's forgiveness for me and allow me time and space for positive change, for looking at myself and my beginnings, for acknowledging the wrongs that I have done, for many apologies to you as God shows me my part in our pain? If you can, I want to start over. I want our love to be like John and Phyllis's, like Jim and Jan's. I want us to open heart to heart, to share history, to share feelings and thoughts, to become one. I am willing to do what it takes to get there."

  Remember our history has colored the way we love. Those four generations before you have told you how to love, and to your partner that may not look or feel like love at all. The reverse is also true—your partner's love may be strange or not identifiable to you.

  Sound confusing? That's why God's love is the only true and consistent love. It is His presence within us that gives us "the hope of glory"—His goodness and mercy. Anything outside of that is counterfeit.

- **Take a long look at your histories, and dump the painful residue.** This is a process of investigating what you brought with you when you entered your relationship, your marriage. What attitudes were handed to you by previous generations, what attitudes did you adopt as a result of personal injuries you have experienced? Perhaps you'd better think about joining one of the actual recovery programs, or at least write down what you learn from others about your heritage and what hardships you have endured that have created not only your attitudes, but your behaviors as well.

Your attitudes and behaviors can and will change as you empty the old pain and the bitterness and resentments that have resulted. You do this as you write in letter form, as if you were writing a letter to be sent to the one who either intentionally or not intentionally wounded you. In the letter you state the reason you are writing: to get rid of the resentment and the effects of it that you have carried for so long. You write that you want to share the pain you felt then, the pain you still feel, and the way that incident or those incidents have affected you, your feelings, thoughts, attitudes, and behaviors ever since the event(s). Lay it all out in that letter. You don't have to be harsh and cruel. Simply and sincerely let your feelings and thoughts be known. Then, having emptied the garbage can full of painful memories, tell the reader that you are choosing to let it all go now, because you have emptied the trash. Then outline how your life will now be different since you have emptied the pain.

You can then take the letter to your mate and read aloud what you have written. If you don't feel you're quite ready for that with your partner just yet, then take it to a close friend of the same gender as yourself, a pastor or a counselor. Read out loud what your hand has written. In so doing, your eyes read the words your hands have written, your ears hear your voice speak the words your hand has written. Your mind and your heart hear the words and your decision to release the bitterness, anger, or resentment you have held onto for dear life. You are committing to yourself and to the hearer, the changes that emptying your old junk will facilitate.

Then take the letter with you. Do whatever you choose with it—burn it, shred it, flush it, or keep it hidden in a safe place. Some have even rolled it tightly or shredded it, stuffed it inside a balloon, blown up the balloon and let it go. Just keep writing the letters until you've done one for every person who has offended you. Sure it'll keep you busy, but you'll be dumping the resentment you've been carrying around. You'll have a much lighter load!

- **If you haven't shared any of this with your partner, do so!** Your partner in life has the right to know the story behind the person. It is amazing how shame can cause us to cover up experiences that we feel will cause others to reject us. But the truth is that your partner always can sense that some kind of dividing wall exists when old

135

memories come between you both. Amazingly, when we began to share with each other the truth of what we (Ron and Nancy) each had experienced before we knew each other, rejection, physical and emotional abuse and even sexual abuse, an amazing weight was removed from us both. We finally began to understand the cause of behaviors we had dumped on each other, causing pain.

Here the **reason** for behavior comes to light, rather than continuing to live in the darkness of the cover-up. And you know what? The unveiling of the secrets of our past caused a new layer of hardened heart to be removed. We each felt especially loved because something very intimate had been disclosed by and about the person we love. That will be your experience too, as you do this work.

- **Begin the heart-opening/softening process.** This happens in a two-way exchange between you and your mate. You give what you know and have learned about how your past has orchestrated your present. You hide nothing that will help to explain who you have been. There are no excuses (cover-ups) for your attitudes and behaviors, but there are reasons (set-ups). Just because you've been set up in the past, does not mean that you need to stay where you've been. It's time to do as Ephesians 4: 31 and 32 demand:

"And do not grieve the Holy Spirit of God, in whom you were sealed for the day of redemption. Get rid of all bitterness, rage and anger, brawling and slander, along with every form of malice."

Verse 32 outlines what comes next:

"Be kind and compassionate to one another, forgiving each other, just as in Christ God forgave you."

That sounds like we need to get rid of the old junk so that we can be kind and compassionate (feeling, empathetic, concerned, considerate, caring, gentle and benevolent), doesn't it?

- **Listen carefully.** Since this is a two-way exchange, your mate listens—actively listens. This means that the children are in bed, the TV is off, there's no puttering happening. It is just two people, sitting together, honestly sharing and hearing each other. The hearing is extremely important because, in childhood, many of us were never heard or felt that we were heard. Perhaps you have never been able to tell your story—your experiences. Maybe no one ever cared to hear your feelings. It could be that you even denied or froze your feelings because they were too painful. This is the time to thaw them out, to hold them in your heart and hands, actually feeling them, and through your tears share them with the one with whom you have chosen to share your life.

- **Make no value judgments.** Feelings are neither right nor wrong. They just are, because they are based on your history. And if they are yours or your partner's, they are real. No one should talk you out of them. You are the only one who can do that, and you do it by acknowledging their existence, sharing them with a listener, and then letting them dissipate.

   Make it a practice to share daily with your partner. Once intimate conversing becomes a habit, you will eagerly anticipate your time together for communicating. Figure out the very best time for you to share, a time when you can both concentrate, hearing each other completely, and often that means hearing *between* the lines!

   We usually spend special time with each other in the morning. We get up, and go to the small library off our kitchen. We sit across from each other with our hot beverage in hand, and we listen, we share, we plan, we discuss, we bounce ideas back and forth; we connect. Being semi-retired, there are other times in the day when we are together—at meals, writing, creating, dealing with scheduling issues or other corporate matters—but those early morning hours are most precious.

   Sometimes when we go to bed, we lay in each other's arms and talk, or we lay looking at each other and talking like we did last night—about Johnny and Phyllis, about how hard it is to see him suffer, and to see her suffering, too, while he slowly slips away. We hold each other knowing that death is inevitable, that sickness will come, that the heartaches of others will show up on our doorstep, that one day we will have to say good-bye to each other, unless the Lord comes before then. And so we cherish the moments.

Let's get real now . . . does this mean that there is never a disagreement, a disappointment or a spat? We'd be lying if we said that was the case. Sometimes we just snip at each other, and sometimes we recognize it and often we don't. But it's not a big deal. We're human, after all. Many snips we just let pass because they aren't a hill we want to die on. For others we apologize, forgive each other, and let it go. None last longer than a few minutes. What's the sense of creating mountains out of molehills? We know another truth too that has become a slogan we believe sincerely and take into account regularly:

"With every period of exhaustion, there is a corresponding period of depression that goes to our weakest point at that moment."

It's a motto we have written indelibly in our brains and have often considered embroidering and placing in a framed picture on the wall. Many have benefited by it through our years of ministry. Now as we get older and our energy isn't quite what it was a few years ago, we have to remind ourselves often, and we do. Consider doing that embroidery or typing it in a fancy print and hanging it in a conspicuous place on your wall.

With every period of exhaustion
there is a corresponding
period of depression, which goes to
our weakest point
at that moment.
Take a nap!

Many arguments could be avoided if we would take this truth into account. In reality, those weak moments are simply about our old selfish natures wanting to survive, so we must remind ourselves of that also.

- **Look at the world and your life through rose-colored glasses.** What good does it do you to sit in your chair, stare at the wall or the TV, moaning and groaning about the terrible cards life has dealt you? If you do that, your life has only one direction to go and it'll be toward more negative, more miserable, more pain and sickness, and perpetual aloneness. Who wants to hear someone moan and groan all the time? If you find yourself stuck here, perhaps it's generational, and it's time that you—your generation makes the change.

  Recall the many stories of people who have overcome seemingly insurmountable odds to enjoy q quality life. Some are born without limbs, others born with devastating abnormalities, yet they have succeeded in making life pleasant and enjoyable. Recently a young Japanese man, born blind, won the Van Cliburn International Piano Competition held in Houston, Texas. He was ushered onto the platform in the final competition by the conductor of the orchestra that was to accompany him.

The conductor had asked, "How will you know the downbeat when you can't see my baton?"

The young pianist replied, "I can hear you breathe. I will know."

And sure enough, he knew. He had a hurdle, but he jumped over it by exaggerating what he could do—he could hear, and as a result played the most difficult of all compositions, Rachmaninoff's "Rack Three," and won!

- **Date, Date, Date!!! Time just for the two of you is VERY IMPORTANT!** We have always made it a practice to take time just for us. Early in our marriage, before the children came along, we planned day trips. We never had a lot of money because of college expenses, but even if it meant going out to a little sub sandwich place and sharing a sandwich and a root beer, we did that. We would take a drive to the lake, put gas in the car, enough to get us to a dairy for an ice cream (of course back then gas was 19 cents a gallon!) After the children came along, we would take them for a weekend to visit Grandma and Grandpa and we would run off to Bee Bee's Dairy for a chocolate ice cream cone, if even for only an hour. We would head north to New Hampshire in the autumn, stop along the way for a few fresh apples and a hunk of cheese, munching as we drove and enjoying the brilliantly colored maple trees. When the children were school age, we used time during their school hours to visit church members, and always managed a bit of time just for us. Our graduate degrees afforded us the opportunity to travel some, so for research we would take a trip to a library or even travel to meet an expert in our field for an interview. On the day we had our most classes, we would go to Boston in the morning, and "people watch" at Faneuil Hall or lay on a blanket by the Charles River, watching the boaters and munching on cheese and crackers. We would take fancy glasses and a bottle of non-alcoholic wine, and would sometimes read to each other or do homework together.

  In one church we pastored every day we received a very early morning phone call. Seldom could we get back to sleep, so once in a while we would throw on some clothes and go to a corner coffee shop for a muffin and tea.

When we left Johnny's beside to fly home (a very early morning flight) we went to dinner at a German restaurant in Milwaukee—just a bit of nostalgia for German Ron, and a place to "take a breath" and enjoy each other's company. We had much to talk about after two day's visit with Phyllis and Johnny. Even in the hardest of times, we have made time just to be together. Words don't always need to be said; just physical presence is sometimes comforting enough.

And still in our Golden Years, we date. A drive onto roads we've never seen, a lunch at our favorite 2 Scoops (an ice cream, soup and sandwich shop here in our town), an hour on our deck overlooking the waterfall shaped arroyo, where we have an actual waterfall when it rains.

Sometime our "date" is late at night in our hot tub, where we get to look at abundant stars and feel the water's soothing warmth. Whenever it is, it is welcomed and cherished, and we'll do it forever!

Moral of the story?

Steal any minutes or hours you can to spend time alone with your sweetheart!

- **Find a goal together, a purpose. Something outside of yourself.** Don't do it for self-gain, for making money, or for patting yourselves on the back. Do it because you truly care to give back to God who gave you life, by caring for others.

When two dogs lay beside the fireplace with nothing to do, with no goal or purpose but to just be comfortable, they start snipping and growling at each other. But give them a joy to do, a load to pull, and they will get in line to be harnessed and work together as a team. Humans aren't much different. Let them discover than their purpose is about giving, not getting; let them discover a way that they can use their gifts to give to others, and hand in hand they will labor together for the greater good of others.

What is your goal as a couple? Is it just to buy that house on the hill, the cottage at the beach, that big new SUV, or to put your kids through an Ivy League University, so that you can brag? Wouldn't you be better off to live in a modest home, drive a modest car, and use a percentage of you income to teach your children how to reach out to be a blessing to others? Have you ever served at a soup kitchen? Have you been on a mission trip to build a church or an orphanage? Have you taught a helpful class to people in your community? Think about doing some kind of community service to bless others, and you'll find yourselves spending less time complaining and finding fault with your mate.

- **Share your heart, share your body:** In all you have read so far, communication has been a major component for marital success. As it relates to the sexual intimacy of marriage, communication is a far more significant element than is technique, frequency, and positioning. The verbal sharing of love and adoration of the mate, at any and every time of the day or night rather than just at bedtime or as a prelude to sex, creates an environment of acceptance and openness.

   Many couples have a "knock down, drag out" fight and moments later are having sex. But it makes such little sense to demean a mate, to call her names, to disrespect who he is, to accuse and blame, and expect that an hour of sex will erase all the words, all the unkindness. Putdowns, sarcasm, derogatory comments are all emotionally abusive, and to be sure, emotional abuse is NOT good foreplay! If a woman is degraded and humiliated by her partner, why would she want to give of herself to someone who really doesn't love and cherish her?

   Especially in the area of sexuality, it is wise to have a discussion before the wedding night. But if you happen to be already married, have the discussion NOW. Share what you expect, what you'd like, how often, what signals to use indicating your interest, and so forth. Scripture makes it clear that the "church" (that's you and us) is the "Bride" (the Woman), and Jesus Christ is the Bridegroom.

   In the fifth chapter of Ephesians, instructions are given to man and wife. The man, the husband is to love the woman, the wife, as Christ loves the church, and gave up His life for her. It further states that a woman is to submit to and respect her husband. Unfortunately, many people and clergy use the word submit as a means of controlling the wife, rather than how it was meant. If this text was read properly, any woman alive would say she was willing to submit to a man who had the characteristics of Jesus Christ!

- **Do not neglect hugs, Kisses and Gentle Love Pats:** Remember when you were dating your partner? Probably you, like thousands of others, couldn't keep your hands off each other. You held hands most of the time, you hugged as often as possible, and kissed every time you could. When you passed by each other, you brushed your hand across his shoulder, you patted his arm. Early on in your marriage, you loved to lie in his arms. You played with her long, flowing hair.

What happened? When did you last go for a walk together and hold hands all the way? How long has it been since you held her in your arms until you fell asleep? When was the last time you sat on his lap, rubbed his shoulders or back, or surprised him with a romantic kiss?

Nancy: One of the strongest cravings of humankind is the want of tender touch. Years ago when I was a full-time R.N., we bathed our hospitalized patients and gave them at least one backrub during each eight-hour shift. I am convinced that our patients required less pain medication and improved quicker because of the caring touch offered by the nursing staff. Today that kind of caring is almost nonexistent in our busy and often understaffed hospitals, and I believe that the patients suffer because of it.

It has been proven that sick or premature babies do better, and heal quicker when they are tenderly stroked or held. All of the skin's nerve endings come alive and are soothed. The circulation of life-giving blood is increased, and a baby's sense of well-being is enhanced.

The same is true of the elderly, who in many cases go long periods of time without contact. A dying patient feels the warmth of physical connection and is comforted by the caring presence of a loved one or a nurse. How important to keep up that tender caressing, those hugs and kisses, so that when our time of death approaches we will be comforted again and again by the kiss or the caress that we recognize as that of our beloved.

- **Never use the "D" word:** A wise person once said that neither husband nor wife should ever say the word divorce in reference to their marriage. We believe that she's right!

 Because of the way the mind works, hearing that word as a threat or even a possibility can plant a doubt in the mind. With every disagreement or "fight," that word jumps back into the thinking process and becomes a fear for the future.

 When a couple stands before a pastor, a priest or a judge, he and she repeat the words: *"For better or worse, for richer, for poorer, in sickness and in health, forsaking all others cleave only unto you, 'til death do us part."* Notice, they don't say, *"until I get sick of you or until you disappoint me!"* It's a permanent arrangement. But apparently the words that cross the lips are not the ones recorded in the mind, because divorce is all too simple and easy these days.

The truth is simple: With God all things are possible, including the healing of a marriage in deep trouble. God says that He hates divorce (Mal. 2:16). He commits to us as His bride with no loopholes, no clauses that allow Him to back out if the going gets rough. It's an everlasting commitment. And so it should be with husband and wife. Committed to make the marriage work regardless of the cost, couples can surmount great obstacles to make their marriages sacred, special, and permanent.

Instead of going to a lawyer, go to a counselor. Instead of going to a bar to numb out the pain, go to a recovery group to work through it. Instead of going to violence, go to God for the strength to overcome your own weaknesses.

- **Harden not your heart:** Scripture has much to say about the hardened heart. Like hardened rubber, the hardened heart is hardly pliable, flexible, or workable. God puts the sin of stubbornness up there with rebellion and idolatry (see 1 Sam. 15:23, KJV; NIV). The heart and mind that stubbornly refuses to listen to reason, that are willing to die trying to get their own way, that will not listen to the call, the still small voice of God, is hardened. *"You are a hard and stubborn people"* the Lord tells the Israelites (see Deut. 9:6). He told them this because they refused to listen to Him and follow in His ways. We can be just as stubborn today. We make up our minds that we expect certain things from our mates, and we make them suffer if they don't get what we want. We don't follow God's ways either!

  Harden not your hearts toward your mate. Unless that partner is abusive, do not hold up your hands signaling "Stop." Be willing to give and take, to seek help when either of you feel the need to do so, and be willing to look in the mirror at what you are contributing to the dysfunction in your relationship.

- **Don't try to manufacture love. It's a free gift!** Human beings do not create or manufacture love—they can only open their arms and hearts to receive it from its author. Everything about God is love—His every thought and action toward us stem from love.

When we willingly accept love from God, then the love we offer to others is God's love, the only type that is of value. What we offer is often, "I will love you, say that I love you, endeavor to show love to you—so that you will love me."

Nancy: I remember it well. I was packing to move to our home here in the mountains. The work was arduous, and emotionally a harder task that I had expected. I was leaving behind the little bit of inheritance I had received from my mother—my kitchen. The money she had left me at her death was put into a beautiful renovation. But the time came that we could not afford that home and our little mountain retirement home, and we had to choose between them. We chose the ideal climate of the mountain region where we now live, with its close proximity to one of our daughters.

Ron was in his study, shredding old, unneeded papers and sorting through items there to be kept or destroyed. As he tells it, *"I felt God speaking to my heart. The message was loud and clear that I should go to the kitchen and give Nancy a hug 'from my heart.' I stubbornly refused. I told myself that Nancy was fine and that thought was silly. But again and again it came, so I finally gave in. When I approached her, I could tell that she was struggling, so I enfolded her in my arms and just held her there, somehow communicating from my heart that I was aware of the struggle she was having. She burst into tears and melted into me. In silence we stood for a while, her quietly weeping, until the tears stopped. It was then that she shared the struggle of leaving behind the gift her mother had left her. Getting out the feelings of guilt and sadness, gave her the courage to continue the packing and move on."*

Nancy: I honestly felt hugged by God that day, and a feeling came over me that everything would be OK. My mother would have understood.

- **Cement yourselves together with Heavenly Glue:** Religion can be a dangerous thing, but spirituality is a whole different ballgame! People fight over religion; the way to practice it, which denomination is best or right, and have even fought to the death to prove their point. Spirituality, however, refers to one's relationship with God, not attendance or membership in a particular church. Spirituality also has to do with our relationship to others. "Whatever you did for one of the least of these brothers of mine, you did for me," Jesus said (Matt. 25:40). He meant that the way we treat others, is the way we are treating Him. And you know what? "Others" includes your mate, your partner, your spouse!

What is the heavenly glue that bonds you together? It is leaving, cleaving, uniting together for a purpose greater than yourselves. It is being naked (vulnerable and open) and not ashamed. Actually marriage is a partnership, a contract, an agreement that you make with God as your witness. God attended your ceremony just like He did at the place of His first miracle on earth, the wedding at Cana of Galilee. At that wedding He turned the water into wine for the benefit of the bride and groom and all those who attended the festivities, but more than that miracle, was the blessing of His presence.

So part of the glue is the presence of God in your marriage. It's God, you, and your mate—a trio, bound together for your blessing, for your happiness and joy. Your marriage is also a blessing to God. It helps to exonerate His name when your well-ordered marriage and family testifies of the great and mighty power of God to cement two people for life. After all, you are from different families and backgrounds, different likes and dislikes, different histories and generational traits, and you are to blend as one. In order for that miracle to occur, there must be a binding agent, one that will never let go, and God is that agent!

Thank Him for bringing you together. Thank Him for your partner, their faults, foibles, and all. Thank Him for allowing and helping you to see yourself clearly and the wounds and scars you brought to your relationship. Rather than begging and pleading for Him to "fix it," thank Him for already doing so, for already being in the process. That way you are concentrating on His adequacy, rather than your inadequacy. It's better for both your brain and your heart to be positive!

- **Keep on, keeping on . . .**

Never ever, not for one moment should you stop working on yourself and your marriage. Just because you brought her roses once ten years ago, is no reason to never, ever do so again. Just because you fixed his favorite meal or baked that apple pie last year, is no reason to not do so—regularly. Just because you have a marriage license is no reason to believe that you have "arrived." Husbands and wives whose marriages last keep working on them, because believe it or not, people change about every ten years. Our thoughts, our feelings, our perspectives on life and love are ever changing, and you will need to keep up, keep current with each other, to make it the best marriage it can be.

Heart to heart connection is an ongoing process. It happens every day, every hour, and it must be nurtured! Keep feeding it what it needs for optimum health— those dates, intimate conversations, sexually intimate moments, spiritual connections are of great importance.

Several years ago, Ron and I went for physical exams. Our doctor was amazed when he looked at the ECG strips that printed out after an electrocardiogram. "Wait a minute!" he gasped, "is this yours Ron, or Nancy's? They looked the same!" Then he lifted them both to the light and put one over the other. "They ARE the same," he shouted. "I've never seen this before!"

"Don't you remember what the Good Book says, Doc?" Ron questioned. "It says in Genesis 2:24 and 25 that 'the two shall be as one.' I guess that's literal as well and emotional."

We have those ECG strips. They are a precious part of our collection of special mementos. That kind of connection can belong to you and your sweetheart too, if you are committed to making your marriage one where you function like Jim and Jan, John and Phyllis, and the many other couples who have chosen to make their marriage a heart-to-heart connection.

God bless you as you commit and move forward to connect, heart to heart!

Write your Commitment here and then read it to out loud to your partner!

EPILOGUE

"The Bottom Line"

Everybody wants to be happy in life; to have loving intimacy with a partner, a warm and accepting relationship with friends, and intimacy with God. This desire is obtainable!

By now, you have no doubt come to recognize that all of your life experiences, from conception onward, have impacted the way you feel, think, and behave. Most of your behaviors stem from your need to survive and from early developed fear, and many of those behaviors have kept you from the intimacy (in-to-me-see) that you crave.

You can do the work of looking into the mirror and examining your history in *The Journey* or *Binding the Wounds* recovery programs, available at www.fixablelife.com. With a thorough look at yourself, at what set you up to be who you are, and doing the work to remove residual bitterness or resentment, you can live in LOVE rather than FEAR.

Apply the Chapter Ten principles and the others you have learned in this book. Wonderful intimacy can be yours if you will do this. Heaven's power is available. Ultimate intimacy is yours for the obtaining, so long as you are willing to be teachable, to do the work and to count on God's power for the results.

If you are teachable, you are fixable!

Bibliography

Downs, Alan. *The Half-Empty Heart.* New York, 2003

Goleman, Daniel. *Emotional Intelligence.* New York, 1995

Guarneri, Mimi. *The Heart Speaks.* New York, 2006

Hagberg, Janet O. and Robert A. Guelich. *The Critical Journey.* Wisconsin, 2005

Pearsall, Paul. *The Heart's Code.* New York, 1998

"Personality Type, Smoking Habit and Their Interaction as Predictors of Cancer and Coronary Heart Disease," published in *Personality and Individual Differences* 9, (1988): 479-95.

Rohner, Ronald P. and Abdul Khaleque. *Handbook for the Study of Parental Acceptance and Rejection. Connecticut, 2005*

Scarf, Maggie. *Secrets, Lies, Betrayals.* New York, 2004

Takotsubo Cardiomyopathy, or Broken-Heart Syndrome published on-line at this address.

Salim S. Virani, MD, A. Nasser Khan, MD, Cesar E. Mendoza, MD, Alexandre C. Ferreira, MD, and Eduardo de Marchena, MD. Texas Heart Institute, 2007

Siegel, Daniel. The Developing Mind. Guilford Press, 1999

Verny, Thomas R. *Pre-Parenting.* New York, 2002

Verny, Thomas R. *The Secret Life of the Unborn Child.* New York, 1981

CPSIA information can be obtained at www.ICGtesting.com
Printed in the USA
LVOW040347160312

273217LV00002B/65/P